God's Promises

God's Promises

BY SALLY MICHAEL

P&R
PUBLISHING
P.O. BOX 817 • PHILLIPSBURG • NEW JERSEY 08865-0817

ISBN: 978-1-59638-432-3 (pbk)
ISBN: 978-1-59638-560-3 (ePub)
ISBN: 978-1-59638-559-7 (Mobi)

Page design and typesetting by Dawn Premako

Printed in the United States of America

Library of Congress Cataloging-in-Publication Data

Michael, Sally, 1953-
 God's promises / by Sally Michael ; [illustrations by Fred Apps].
   p. cm.
 Includes bibliographical references.
 ISBN 978-1-59638-432-3 (pbk.)
 1. God (Christianity)--Promises--Juvenile literature. I. Apps, Fred. II. Title.
 BT180.P7M53 2012
 231.7--dc23
                              2012006980

Dedicated to my grandson,
Joshua Michael Steward.

May you trust in the sure promises of God
because you trust in the Promise Keeper.

Your kingdom is an everlasting kingdom,
and your dominion endures through all generations.

The Lord is faithful to all his promises
and loving toward all he has made.
—Psalm 145:13 (NIV)

Contents

Preface

God is not man, that he should lie, or a son of man, that he should change his mind. Has he said, and will he not do it? Or has he spoken, and will he not fulfill it? —Numbers 23:19

God's promises of blessing are like presents to His people. They are undeserved, but given because God is good and loving. People break promises, but not God. His Word is sure and trustworthy. It stands from age to age, unchanging and unbroken. What He has said, He will do.

God's promises are precious, and they are powerful. Behind them stands the all-powerful, unchanging, wise, loving, patient, good, faithful, sovereign Creator and Ruler of the Universe. He watches over His Word and accomplishes all His purposes.

God has given His children these precious promises to remind us of His goodness and to strengthen our faith when we are weak. They will assure you of His care, comfort you in sorrow, replace weakness with strength, remind you of His presence, and bring courage when you are fearful. Cling to them like a vine clings to a tree. Wrap your arms around them and don't let them go. Trust in them without wavering, for they are the very Word of God Almighty.

When your faith is weak, look up to God, your loving and strong Father, not down at your circumstances. Trust His wise plans for your life and His ways and means of bringing about His purposes for you. He never makes mistakes, and His heart is always for His people. Stand on His promise that He will do good to you . . . always . . . and forever.

> I believe that I shall look upon the goodness of the Lord
> in the land of the living!
> Wait for the Lord;
> be strong, and let your heart take courage;
> wait for the Lord! (Psalm 27:13–14)

Introduction
How to Use This Book

This book was written to give parents an opportunity to present solid truth to their children and to encourage real-life application of the truth.

Relational

Children receive more encouragement to learn when truth is presented by a trusted individual. Your positive, relational parent-child commitment will be a real benefit when you sit down together to read this book. Your time together over the Word should be positive, affirming, and loving.

Interactive

There is a greater impact when an individual discovers truth, instead of just hearing it presented. Many questions have been incorporated into the text of this book to encourage your child to wonder and think critically. The process of discovery will be circumvented if you don't give your child adequate time to think and respond. After asking a question, wait for a response. If your child has difficulty, ask the question a different way or give a few hints.

Questions and responses can be springboards for more questions and discovery as you interact with your child's mind and heart. The Holy Spirit is the real teacher, so depend on Him to give both you and your child thoughts and truths to explore together, and to bring the necessary understanding. Take the time to work through each story at a leisurely pace—giving time for interaction and further dialogue. The goal should be to get the material into the child, not just to get the child through the material.

Understandable

These stories have been written with attention given to explaining difficult or potentially new concepts. Some of these concepts may take time for your child to digest. Allow your child to ponder new truths. Read the story more than once, allowing the truth to be better understood and integrated into your child's theological framework. At times, have your child read parts of the lesson, giving an opportunity for visual learning.

Because vocabulary can be child-specific, define the particular words foreign to your child. Retell difficult sections in familiar wording, and ask questions to be sure your child understands the truth being taught.

Theological

More than just acquainting your child with the promises of God, this book is building a biblical theology beneath your child. As your child begins to correctly understand who God is and how He interacts with the world, he or she won't just have a vague notion of God, but will be able to relate to the God of the Bible.

Because the Word of God has convicting and converting power, Bible texts are quoted word-for-word in some parts. Some of these verses may be beyond the child's understanding, so you may need to explain unfamiliar words or thoughts. Even though clear comprehension may be difficult, hearing the Word itself is a means the Holy Spirit can use to encourage faith in your child (Romans 10:17). Do not minimize the effectual influence of God's Word in the tender souls of children.

Since the Word of God is living and active, allow the child to read the Bible verses as much as possible. Also, encourage your child to memorize some of the verses so he or she can meditate on them at other times.

The gospel is presented numerous times throughout the book. Use this as an opportunity to share God's work of grace in your life, and to converse with your child about his or her spiritual condition. Be careful not to confuse spiritual interest with converting faith and give premature assurances to your child. Fan the flames of gospel-inspired conviction and tenderness toward the sacrificial love of Jesus without prematurely encouraging your child to pray "the sinner's prayer."[1]

Application

Understanding the truth is essential, but insufficient. Truth must also be embraced in the heart and acted on in daily life. Often, children cannot make the connection between a biblical truth and real-life application, so you, the parent, must help bridge the gap.

Consider the following quotation by D. Martyn Lloyd-Jones:

> We must always put things in the right order, and it is Truth first. . . . The heart is always to be influenced through the understanding—the mind, then the heart, then the will. . . . But God forbid that anyone should think that it ends with the intellect. It starts there, but it goes on. It then moves the heart and finally the man yields his will. He obeys, not grudgingly or unwillingly, but with the whole heart. The Christian life is a glorious perfect life that takes up and captivates the entire personality.[2]

Spend a few days or even a week on each promise. Reread the story, discuss the truths, and follow the suggestions in the Learning to Trust God section. Most importantly, help your child to see that God is who He says He is, and to act in response to the truth. Point out God's involvement in daily life, and thank Him for being true to His promises.

1. Some excellent resources for parents regarding the salvation of children can be found at www.children desiringgod.org. Resources include: a booklet, *Helping Children Understand the Gospel*; and two seminars from the 2007 conference, "'How Great a Salvation': Leading Children to a Solid Faith" and "Presenting the Gospel to Children."

2. D. Martyn Lloyd-Jones, *Spiritual Depression* (Grand Rapids: William B. Eerdmans, 1965), 61–62.

Prayer

Ultimately, our efforts are effective only if the Holy Spirit breathes on our teaching and quickens it to the heart. Pray not only before going through the stories, but also in the succeeding days, that your child would see God's character and respond in faith to Him.

Note: *God's Promises* is a topical study with stories ordered in a logical progression. The introductory story acquaints children with promises, followed by two stories identifying the recipients of God's promises—believers and unbelievers. An explanation of conditional and unconditional promises is presented next to show children the difference between these two kinds of promises. Stories 5 and 6 assure children that God's promises are trustworthy because God, the Promise Giver, is trustworthy, thus showing the connection between God's character and His Word.

The following seventeen stories expose children to specific promises God has made to believers, starting with two that explain how a person inherits the promises through salvation. The book ends with three stories challenging children to trust in God's promises.

Promises Are Like Presents

What's the difference between "We should go to a baseball game," and "I promise to take you to a baseball game"?

A promise is when a person says he will or will not do something, and he really means it. He is not just thinking about it. He has decided to do it. You can count on it. He will do it.

Suppose your mom says, "I promise I will not pull your tooth out. I will only wiggle your tooth to see how loose it is." If she says that, she is telling you something she will do—wiggle your tooth—and something she will not do—pull it out. You do not need to worry that your mom will pull out your tooth, because she has made a promise. You can be sure of it.

The Bible is full of God's promises—things God has said that He will or will not do. These are promises you can count on for sure. Some of God's promises tell us what He will do. For example:

I will instruct you and teach you in the way you should go. (Psalm 32:8)

Some promises tell us how things are for the Christian, the person who is trusting in Jesus:

[Nothing] in all creation, will be able to separate us from the love of God in Christ Jesus our Lord. (Romans 8:39)

Nothing can ever take away God's love for those who trust in Jesus. God loves His children . . . everywhere . . . all the time . . . forever! He *promises* this, so we can be sure that this is really true, that God really is like this and will always be like this.

Sometimes God's promises are found in things He tells us about Himself. When God tells us who He is, He is making a promise about what He is like and what He will do. For example:

The LORD is merciful and gracious,
    slow to anger and abounding in steadfast love. (Psalm 103:8)

Since this verse tells us what God is like, it also has in it a *promise* about God. God is kind and doesn't become angry quickly. He is patient and full of love. This

is who God says He is. Because God is kind and patient, He is promising to act with kindness and patience. This is what He will do.

What does God promise by saying this about Himself?

> The LORD is good to all,
>   and his mercy is over all that he has made. (Psalm 145:9)

God says He is good and kind. This is what He says about Himself. But God is also promising here to show goodness and kindness to EVERYONE!

This is a wonderful promise! It is like a present. All of God's promises to bless us—to do good to us—are gifts. We don't deserve them. God doesn't have to give them to us. He gives them because He is good and loving.

Do you like to get presents? What is one present that you really liked? You will find that God's promises are the very best presents of all. Not only are God's promises wonderful, but they don't wear out or break—they are forever!

The Bible is full of God's promises—things God has said that He will or will not do. Promises that tell us what God is like and who He will always be. Promises you can count on. God's promises are sure.

In this book, you will discover some of God's many promises. They will be like opening wonderful presents—gifts from God that we don't deserve, which show us how good and loving He is.

Here is a verse for you to remember as you read this book and discover God's gift of His wonderful promises to His children.

> Every good gift and every perfect gift is from above, coming down from the Father of lights with whom there is no variation or shadow due to change. (James 1:17)

LEARNING TO TRUST GOD

✤ Read James 1:17 again. What does this verse tell you about God? If God never changes, what does this mean about who He is today and about His promises?

✤ Look through your Bible and find some of God's promises. Who is each promise for? How is each promise like a present? Look at one or two promises and thank God for that promise and what it means for your family.

✤ *Activity:* Get a box with a lid (big enough to hold 25 3" x 5" index cards). Wrap the box and lid in very pretty paper, or decorate the box. Make a label that says, "God's Promises," and glue it to the box. Tell someone why God's promises are like presents.

God's Promises to Believers

If your school promises a prize to everyone who reads 10 books, can third graders get the prize? How about fifth graders? Yes, this promise is for everyone in the school. But if a teacher promises her third-grade class a prize for reading 10 books, will the fifth graders get a prize? Why not? Fifth graders won't get a prize because the promise is only for the third-grade class.

Just as our promises are sometimes for everyone and sometimes only for certain people, some of God's promises are for all people and some are only for His children. Some promises are just for one person. Can you think of a time when God made a promise to just one person?

Did you think of these promises?

- God promised David that he would be the king of Israel.[1]
- God promised wisdom, knowledge, wealth, riches, and honor to Solomon.[2]
- God promised Zechariah and Elizabeth that He would give them a son.[3]

God also made a special promise to Abram. He told Abram:

> I will make you exceedingly fruitful, and I will make you into nations, and kings shall come from you. And I will establish my covenant between me and you and your offspring after you throughout their generations for an everlasting covenant, to be God to you and to your offspring after you. (Genesis 17:6–7)

1. 1 Samuel 16:12
2. 2 Chronicles 1:12
3. Luke 1:13

God promised that Abram would be His special child, and that whole nations of peoples would come from Abram. God renamed him "Abraham" and promised to always be his God. But who else is this promise for? It is for Abraham's "offspring."

What does "offspring" mean? Offspring means children born to someone. Maybe you were born to your mom and dad. If so, you are their offspring and you belong to their family. And your offspring—everyone born to you—would be part of the family, too. So is everyone born to your children . . . and everyone born to their children . . . and on and on.

So God's promise to be God and to be good to Abraham was for Abraham. But it was also for everyone in Abraham's family.

God made many special and wonderful promises to the family of Abraham. God made promises to bless them—to be good to them always. He made promises like this one:

For I know the plans I have for you, declares the Lord, plans for welfare and not for evil, to give you a future and a hope. (Jeremiah 29:11)

Isn't this a wonderful promise? It is a special, for-sure promise of God's goodness. God made many promises like this . . . not to everyone, just to the family of Abraham.

But what if you weren't born into the family of Abraham? Does that mean the promises made to Abraham's family are not for you?

There is another way children become part of a family besides being born into the family. Do you know what that is? It's by adoption. What does it mean to be adopted into a family?

In adoption, the head of the family invites someone to be part of the family. He takes care of all the papers that make the adopted person a full member of the family with the same privileges as everyone else in the family.

If someone wants to be part of another family, he can't just decide that he is in the family. He has to be invited into the family and made a family member through adoption.

God invites people into His family, too—through faith in Jesus. We can be adopted into Abraham's family, the family of God, by trusting in Jesus as our Savior. God says that **"it is those of faith who are the sons of Abraham"** (Galatians 3:7). God welcomes those who have Abraham-like faith in Jesus into His family.[4]

> To all who did receive him, who believed in his name, he gave the right to become children of God. (John 1:12)

If you are trusting in Jesus as your Savior, then all the promises to God's people are for you![5] This is good news. Every promise of God to do good to His people can be yours through faith in Jesus Christ.

---

4. Romans 4:16: "That is why it depends on faith, in order that the promise may rest on grace and be guaranteed to all his offspring—not only to the adherent of the law but also to the one who shares the faith of Abraham, who is the father of us all"; Galatians 3:29: "And if you are Christ's, then you are Abraham's offspring, heirs according to the promise."

5. 2 Corinthians 1:20: "For all the promises of God find their Yes in him."

LEARNING TO TRUST GOD

✦ Read the "Ten Essential Truths" in the Appendix and talk about these truths. What does it mean to be a child of Abraham by faith? Are you a child of God?

✦ Write out John 1:12 on an index card and put it in your "God's Promises" box. You may want to decorate the back side of the card like a gift as a reminder that all God's promises are undeserved gifts. Then thank God for the gift of adoption.

✦ *Activity:* Make a booklet to help you remember the "Ten Essential Truths," and explain these truths to someone.

God's Promise to Unbelievers

Who do you give gifts to? Do people often give gifts to those who don't like them? Sometimes they do, but not usually. But every day God gives good gifts to people who don't like Him—even to those who hate him! What are some of the good gifts God gives to those who don't love Him?

The Bible says,

For he makes his sun rise on the evil and on the good, and sends rain on the just and on the unjust. (Matthew 5:45)

What a kind and loving God we have! He is good to those who love Him, and even to those who don't. He gives His rain and sun to EVERYONE!

But God's kindness to those who don't love Him isn't forever. In the end, after having had so much goodness from God, if a person does not trust in Him and turn away from sin and love God most of all, that person will not live forever with God in heaven.

Jesus told a story about what happens to the person who does not love God.[1] In the story, that person was a rich man who lived in a big house, and had very expensive clothes and a lot of delicious food. He didn't love God, and he didn't love others.

The other person in the story was Lazarus. Lazarus was a very poor man who didn't even have enough to eat. He would lie outside the gates to the rich man's big house, wishing he could have the leftover food the rich man didn't eat. He didn't have expensive clothes or live in a big house. But he did have the love of God.

Lazarus died and went to heaven. The rich man died, too. But he didn't go to heaven. He went to hell where there was great pain and suffering. How he

1. Luke 16:19–31

wished for even a drop of cool water in the fiery flames of hell! He thought maybe Lazarus could help him:

And he called out, "Father Abraham, have mercy on me, and send Lazarus to dip the end of his finger in water and cool my tongue, for I am in anguish in this flame." (Luke 16:24)

But a person can't cross over from heaven to hell. Hell is a forever place. There is no end of the pain and suffering there. A person can't leave hell, and no one can help him. So the rich man could not get help, and there was no end to his terrible misery.

Jesus told this story to warn us about hell and the never-ending suffering and pain there so that we would see what life without God is like. After a person dies, there is no way he can change his mind, or cross over from hell to heaven.

God has many wonderful promises of blessing for His children, and even some promises of good to those who don't love Him. But He also has one very terrible promise of punishment for sin for those who don't trust in Jesus. This is the promise of pain and misery in hell.

This is not a "maybe this will happen" thing but a "for sure this will happen" thing. This is a sure promise by the God who rules the whole world and everyone in it. Someday God will judge every person—to decide whether that person lives forever with Him in heaven or suffers forever in hell.

This is what the Bible says about that judging:

Therefore the wicked will not stand in the judgment,
    nor sinners in the congregation of the righteous;
for the LORD knows the way of the righteous,
    but the way of the wicked will perish. (Psalm 1:5–6)

This is the one awful promise God makes to those who do not love Him or trust in Jesus—"the way of the wicked will perish." Perish means die, and hell is a place of death and sadness, suffering, and pain, not a place of joy and love like heaven.

God must punish sin. Each person must either trust in Jesus' payment for his sin on the cross, or pay for it himself in hell. Who will pay for your sin—you or Jesus?

LEARNING TO TRUST GOD

✢ Read Psalm 1. What does this psalm say about the wicked—those who do not love and trust in Jesus? What does it say about the righteous—those who love and trust in Jesus? What promises are made to each?

✢ Write out Psalm 1:5–6 on an index card and put it in your "God's Promises" box. Thank God that He watches over the way of the righteous. Pray for those you know who are not trusting in Jesus for the payment of their sins.

✢ *Activity:* This week, share the good news of Jesus' payment for sin with someone.

Promises with Conditions

If your mother said to you today, "After supper, we will have ice cream," you would probably be quite happy. This is a good promise—especially if you like ice cream!

But suppose she said, "If you eat all your supper, you can have ice cream for dessert." What is different about this promise? Would you know for sure that an ice cream treat is coming? Would you get the ice cream if you did not finish your supper?

The second promise is a promise with a *condition*. There is something that must happen first, or that you must do, to get the promised ice cream. You must eat your supper first.

Some of God's promises are promises with conditions. You must first do something, or something must first happen, before God will do what He has promised. We could call these "if promises," because they sometimes have the word "if" in them. See whether you can find the condition—the thing that a person must do before God will give the promised blessing—in these verses:

> If we confess our sins, he is faithful and just to forgive us our sins and to cleanse us from all unrighteousness. (1 John 1:9)

> For if you forgive others their trespasses, your heavenly Father will also forgive you. (Matthew 6:14)

God will forgive the sins of His people *if* they confess them. First they must confess, then God will forgive. God will forgive our sin *if* we forgive others. The condition is that we must forgive.

Not all "if promises" use the word "if," but they all have a condition—something that a person must do or something that must happen first for God to give what is promised. Here is an "if promise" without an "if":

You keep him in perfect peace
     whose mind is stayed on you,
     because he trusts in you. (Isaiah 26:3)

What must a person do to receive God's promised peace—to keep him free from worry and fear? He must think about God—about how good and great He is. He must remember who God is and trust God to care for him, and then God gives him peace.

If you did not eat all your supper, would your mother have to give you ice cream? Why not? You did not do what you were supposed to do. You did not keep the condition of the promise.

Just as your mother does not have to give you the promised ice cream if you don't eat all your supper, so God does not have to give the promised blessing if we do not do what He says we must do. God, the Ruler of the whole world, has the right to make whatever conditions He wants. And if those conditions are not kept, He does not have to give the blessing.

When you read a promise, you must ask yourself, "Is there something that I must do for the promised blessing to come?" This is very important because God always keeps His promises, but we do not always keep the conditions. If we do not do what God asks in His conditions, we should not expect God to give the good blessing that He has promised to those who keep His conditions.

God freely gives good things to all people, and especially to His children. We don't deserve these blessings—we can't earn them by doing the right thing. But when we keep God's conditions, many of His blessings come to us.

Listen to the "if promise" that God gave to His people in the Old Testament:

And if you faithfully obey the voice of the Lord your God, being careful to do all his commandments that I command you today, the Lord your God will set you high above all the nations of the earth. And all these blessings shall come upon you and overtake you, if you obey the voice of the Lord your God. (Deuteronomy 28:1–2)

God promised Israel many wonderful and good blessings, but some of those promises had conditions—conditions that Israel had to obey to be able to receive the promise of God. God loves to do good to His people, but His people must obey Him, just as you must obey your parents to receive what they have promised if they make a condition.

Do you think the people of Israel always obeyed God or kept His conditions? No, sadly, they did not. So they missed so many of God's good blessings.

God's promises are so good. And His conditions are always good and right. But we must not think that God will give us His good blessing if we do not obey Him and do what He has asked. But what joy there is for us and what blessing is ours if we obey God and follow His ways. He will be our God, and we will be His people!

LEARNING TO TRUST GOD

✤ Read Deuteronomy 30:16–18. What does God promise? What are His conditions? Why is God good and right to give these conditions?

✤ Read Jeremiah 7:23. Talk about some ways that you can "walk in God's ways." Write this verse on an index card and put it in your "God's Promises" box. Memorize the verse and use it to pray for yourself and your family.

✤ *Activity:* Read Matthew 10:32–33. What is the condition and the promised blessing? What does "acknowledge" mean? How can you acknowledge Jesus this week? Pray for courage for each other. Acknowledge God before men, and then share your experience with each other.

God Always Keeps His Promises

I f you turn on the water in your sink, what direction does it flow? Does it ever flow up to the ceiling? No! It never does. It *always* flows down. Always, always, always. It never changes. That is the way it is with God and His promises. God *always, always, always* keeps His promises. He never breaks one of them—ever.

But people sometimes break promises. Some people lie when they make promises and never mean to keep them. However, many people make promises and try to keep them, but they just can't—like when your father says that he will take you to the zoo, but then the car breaks down and you can't go. Your dad didn't know the car would break down, and he didn't know he couldn't keep his promise about the zoo.

Sometimes people break promises because they change their minds—like when a friend promises he will trade his peanut butter sandwich for your ham sandwich . . . and then decides he really does want the peanut butter sandwich and won't trade.

People break promises because they are not strong enough to keep the promise—like when a friend promises to lift you up to a tree branch but can't because he isn't strong enough. Or when your mother promises to make your favorite dessert and then finds that she doesn't have what she needs to make it. And sometimes people forget to keep promises they make.

But God doesn't have any of these problems. Why not?

God is able to keep His promises because He is the Strong Creator of the whole world. He knows everything and is all-powerful. Nothing is too hard for Him. There is nothing God can't do, nothing He doesn't know, and nothing that surprises Him. There is no promise He can't keep.

God never changes His mind. He never lies. And He never forgets anything, including His promises. God is not like people. God is God, perfect in every way.

God is not man, that he should lie
   or a son of man, that he should change his mind.
Has he said, and will he not do it?
   Or has he spoken, and will he not fulfill it? (Numbers 23:19)

What God says He will do, He always does . . . like He did with baby Isaac.

God made a promise to Abram, a *very* important promise.

And I will make of you a great nation, and I will bless you and make your name great, so that you will be a blessing. I will bless those who bless you, and him who dishonors you I will curse, and in you all the families of the earth shall be blessed. (Genesis 12:2–3)

God promised to make a great nation of people to come from Abram. But for that to happen Abram would need to have a child . . . who would have children . . . who would have more children. But Abram and his wife, Sarai, had no child.

They waited and waited. They waited for years. But God did not give them a child. Did God forget His promise or change His mind?

No, God even reminded Abram of His promise,[1] and He gave Abram a new name—Abraham, "father of many nations." He gave Sarai a new name—Sarah, "mother of nations." But still no baby came.

Abraham waited 25 years—until he was an old man, 100 years old! Sarah was 90 years old—much too old to have children. Maybe God wasn't strong enough to give them a baby . . . maybe He didn't know Abraham and Sarah were getting too old to have a baby . . . No! God is God Almighty—nothing is too hard for Him! He knows everything, and He *always* keeps His promises.

So when Abraham was 100 years old, and Sarah was 90, God gave them baby Isaac, just as He promised. And Isaac had children, and those children had children, and those children had children . . . and they became a great nation. Just like God said.

And God made more and more promises to His people . . . hundreds and hundreds of them! The Bible is full of God's promises. Not one of them will be broken! God is God Almighty, the all-knowing, all-powerful, never-lying, never-forgetting God who *always* keeps His promises.

1. Genesis 15:5–6

His promises are for sure, and they are forever!

The grass withers, the flower fades,
  but the word of our God will stand forever. (Isaiah 40:8)

LEARNING TO TRUST GOD

✢ More than 700 years after God's promise to Abram to make a great nation, Joshua spoke to this great nation. Read Joshua 23:14. What does this verse tell you about God?

✢ Write out Numbers 23:19 and Isaiah 40:8 on an index card and put it in your "God's Promises" box. Thank God that He *always* keeps His promises. What promises from the Bible can you think of? Remember that these are just a few of the hundreds of promises God has made.

✢ *Activity:* Write out Isaiah 40:8 on a note card. Then explain it in your own words. Plant some flower or grass seeds in a pot. When the plant begins to grow, bring your card and the plant to someone who needs encouragement to trust God. Pray for him or her and remind that person of God's promises.

Trusting God's Promises

Like he did for Abram, God promised a baby to another man in the Bible. Do you know who that was? He was a priest, and he, too, was an old man. If you guessed Zechariah, then you are right. One day in the temple, God sent an angel to Zechariah to give him this promise:

Do not be afraid, Zechariah, for your prayer has been heard, and your wife Elizabeth will bear you a son, and you shall call his name John. And you will have joy and gladness, and many will rejoice at his birth, for he will be great before the Lord. (Luke 1:13–15)

What a wonderful promise! Zechariah would have a son who would bring him great joy. But even more important, this son would have a strong faith in God and would be an important prophet.

Would Zechariah believe this wonderful promise from God? If he really trusted in God's promise—if he was sure that God *always* keeps His promises—what might Zechariah do?

Maybe he would be so happy and excited that he would run and tell all his friends that God would give him a special baby. Maybe he would go home and tell Elizabeth to start making some baby clothes! Or maybe he would start making a cradle for the baby. Or . . . maybe he would just sit down and thank God for being so good and for being a God who always keeps His promises.

But Zechariah didn't do any of these things. He didn't run out to tell his friends or start making a baby cradle because Zechariah did not trust God's promise. He didn't believe God would give him a child. He didn't think about how great God is—that He can do anything and that He does all that He says He will do.

Instead of seeing how big God is, Zechariah saw how old he was . . . and how old Elizabeth was. He did not have faith in God's greatness or trust in God's promise. Because Zechariah did not trust God's promise, there was a consequence. God said to him:

And behold, you will be silent and unable to speak until the day that these things take place, because you did not believe my words, which will be fulfilled in their time. (Luke 1:20)

Zechariah would not be able to talk until the birth of the baby. He couldn't tell about the angel, explain why he couldn't talk, or even say what he wanted for supper. Worst of all, Zechariah couldn't talk to his friends or Elizabeth about God's wonderful promise of a son who would be great before the Lord and give them great joy. He couldn't talk about the wonderful promise that God would keep at just the right time, just as He said He would because God *always* keeps His promises.

Did God keep His promise to Zechariah? YES! God *always* keeps His promises, and Elizabeth did have a baby . . . and he was a boy. His name was John, and he was great before the Lord. Baby John became John the Baptist, who announced the coming of Jesus, God's own Son.

Our God is a great promise-keeping God. So we can trust in all His promises. To trust in His promises is to act, believing that the promise will happen, like Abram did:

Now the Lord said to Abram, "Go from your country and your kindred and your father's house to the land that I will show you. And I will make of you a great nation, and I will bless you and make your name great, so that you will be a blessing." (Genesis 12:1–2)

God promised that He would make from Abram a great nation in a new land. So what did Abram do? He trusted God's promise, packed all his things, took his wife and nephew and others, and started out for a new land. He *acted* in faith. Abram obeyed God because he trusted God and His promise.

By faith Abraham obeyed when he was called to go out to a place that he was to receive as an inheritance. And he went out, not knowing where he was going. By faith he went to live in the land of promise, as in a foreign land, living in tents with Isaac and Jacob, heirs with him of the same promise. (Hebrews 11:8–9)

Our great promise-keeping God kept His promise and made from Abram the great nation of Israel.

Zechariah could not announce the coming of his own son because he did not trust the promise of God. Abram trusted the promise of God and obeyed God, leaving his home to go to the land of God's promise. He acted on God's promise because He trusted our great promise-keeping God and His promise.

Do you want to be like Zechariah, or like Abram?

LEARNING TO TRUST GOD

✢ Read Hebrews 11:1. What does assurance mean? What does "the conviction of things not seen" mean? Explain this verse in your own words. Write out the verse and put it on the cover of your "God's Promises" box.

✢ Read Hebrews 11. Make a chart listing each person, what he believed, and how he *acted* in faith.[1] Pray for a Hebrews 11 kind of faith.

✢ *Activity:* Dad or mom, make a promise to your child this week.[2] Note each time your child acts with confidence in your promise. Then, keep the promise as you are able.

---

1. This is a bit tricky, and parents may have to "fill in some of the blanks" for their children.
2. Make sure the promise is one that your child has numerous opportunities to act on.

Salvation . . . for Everyone Who Calls

At one time in America, children learned the alphabet by reciting a short poem for each letter. The poem for the letter "A" was: "In Adam's fall, we sinned all."[1] So they learned the letter "A," but they also learned a very important truth—that we are all sinners. When Adam disobeyed God in the garden of Eden, he passed on to all people a sin nature that leads to death and hell.[2]

The Good News is that one man's obedience and sinlessness brought salvation to the world.[3] Do you know who that one man is? Jesus, God's own Son, came to earth to save man from the punishment of sin and to give those who believe in Him a new heart. Salvation through faith in Jesus is not earned, and can't be bought. It is a free gift from God, because God is good and kind to undeserving sinners.

God is kind to undeserving sinners like the thief on the cross. Do you remember that story?

Although Jesus came to bring God's greatest gift to man, the gift of salvation, most people didn't believe in Him. They didn't believe He is God's Son who came to save sinners. They were so angry at Jesus that they wanted Him killed. So Pilate, the governor, gave them permission to crucify—to kill—Jesus on a cross.

Only the worst criminals were crucified—the worst criminals *and* the perfect Jesus who never did anything wrong, never had a bad attitude, and only did good.

Two men were crucified with Jesus. Do you remember who they were? They were robbers who deserved to be crucified. But Jesus did not do anything wrong.

1. From *The New England Primer*, published in 1690 by Benjamin Harris.
2. Romans 5:12
3. Romans 5:18–19

One man knew this, but the other man mocked Jesus—he didn't believe that Jesus was God, or that He could save them.

The robber who knew he deserved to die spoke to Jesus, too—but he didn't make fun of Jesus when he spoke. What did he say to God's own Son, who came to bring salvation to men? What could a very bad man expect from the sinless Jesus?

Jesus, remember me when you come into your kingdom. (Luke 23:42)

What did Jesus say to this sinful man? Did Jesus help the robber on the cross?

And he said to him, "Truly, I say to you, today you will be with me in Paradise." (Luke 23:43)

Jesus promised to bring the thief on the cross to heaven! Why would Jesus die to save sinners . . . even a robber? Jesus is kind and merciful, and He came to save sinners. God's promise to undeserving sinners is:

And it shall come to pass that everyone who calls upon the name of the Lord shall be saved. (Acts 2:21)

"Everyone who calls upon the name of the Lord" . . . even robbers . . . will be saved.

Does this mean that every person will be saved from punishment for his or her sins and go to heaven? No, this is a promise with a condition. What is the condition?

Sinful men must "call on the name of the Lord"—they must admit that they are sinners deserving of punishment. They must trust Jesus to forgive their sins, turn away from sin, and believe that Jesus is God's Son who offers God's gift of salvation. And *everyone, everyone* who calls on the Lord will be saved.

One robber was saved—the one who called out to Jesus for help. The other wasn't—he did not call out to Jesus; he did not trust in Jesus.

"In Adam's fall, we sinned all" . . . and we all deserve God's anger and punishment in hell. Everyone is either like the robber who called on Jesus to save him, or like the one who depended on himself and would not trust Jesus. Which one are you like?

If you come to Jesus, seeing your sin and trusting Jesus to pay for your sin and give you a new heart, Jesus has a special promise for you:

All that the Father gives me will come to me, and whoever comes to me I will never cast out. (John 6:37)

LEARNING TO TRUST GOD

✤ Read about another man who called on Jesus in Luke 19:1–10. Did Zacchaeus deserve forgiveness? How did Jesus treat Zacchaeus? How did coming to Jesus change Zacchaeus?

✤ Write out Acts 2:21 and John 6:37 on an index card and put it in your "God's Promises" box. Pray and thank God for His free gift of salvation to all who come to Jesus in faith.

✤ *Activity:* Read Romans 10:14–15. What can your family do this week to bring the Good News to someone, or to send someone to teach lost sinners about Jesus? Come up with a plan and do it.

Faithful to Forgive

When someone is mean to us—hurts us or says unkind things—how do we usually feel about that at first? We often feel angry . . . and we want to hurt him back.

But Jesus is not like that. When He was on the cross, men made fun of Him. They spit on Him and called Him names. Before that, they beat Him and pushed a crown of sharp thorns on His head. They were mean and cruel to Jesus, but Jesus was not mean to them. He did not want to hurt them. Instead,

Jesus said, "Father, forgive them, for they know not what they do." (Luke 23:34)

Instead of wanting to hurt them, Jesus loved them. He asked God to forgive their sins—not to punish them for their sins. He did not send angels to hurt or kill them. He did not call them names, yell at them, or spit back at them. He saw their sin—their anger, unkindness, and hatred for Him. But His heart was full of mercy—kindness to undeserving sinners. So He prayed for them.

When Jesus did this, He was also showing us His Father's heart. God is eager to forgive sin. He likes to forgive more than He likes to punish.[1] Jesus told us a story so that we would understand this. It is called the story of the Prodigal Son.[2] Do you know that story?

A father had two sons—the younger son was rebellious. He didn't like his father's ideas, rules, or way of doing things. He wanted his own way, and he wanted to be free from his father. So he took the money his father gave him and left home to live as he wanted. He did all kinds of bad things and wasted his father's money.

1. Ezekiel 33:11
2. Luke 15:11–32

When he had no money left and had all kinds of problems, he saw how wrong he had been. He knew that his father's way was best. So he went back to his father.

Do you know what his father did when he saw him? He ran to him, hugged him, and kissed him. The father had been eagerly waiting for his son, and was so happy that his son had come home.

And the son said to him, "Father, I have sinned against heaven and before you. I am no longer worthy to be called your son." (Luke 15:21)

The son admitted his sin. He knew he was a sinner and did not deserve his father's kindness. But his father forgave him. He excused his sin. He did not punish his son for it, but let it go. Instead of yelling at his son for wasting his money, he gave his son beautiful clothing, a ring, and shoes . . . and had a party for him!

Jesus told this story so that we would know that God, the Father, is like the father in the story. He loves to forgive sin and has given us a wonderful promise of forgiveness:

If we confess our sins, he is faithful and just to forgive us our sins and to cleanse us from all unrighteousness. (1 John 1:9)

Does God forgive everyone's sin? No. This is a promise with a condition. What is the condition? We must confess our sin. This means that we must admit we are sinners who have done wrong things. We have had sinful thoughts and bad attitudes. We must see that our sin is terrible, and that we deserve God's anger and punishment. If we do, God's wonderful promise is that he will forgive that sin and erase it for us:

> I, I am he
>> who blots out your transgressions for my own sake,
>> and I will not remember your sins. (Isaiah 43:25)

God erases the sin of those who repent—those who admit their sin and turn away from it. Have you ever used an eraser to get rid of a mistake? What happens to your mistake when you do that? That's the way it is when God erases or blots out our sin. When he does that, our sin is gone. God's promise to forgive those who confess their sins is a wonderful and undeserved gift.

The older son in the story was mad that his father forgave his brother. He did not see that he was also a sinner. He thought he was so good that he did not need forgiveness. So he did not confess his sin—admit that he was a sinner, or that he was jealous, angry, or unkind and needed forgiveness.

Only one brother saw his sin. When he did, he received the gift of forgiveness.

Will you be like the older brother who thought he was so good, or will you be like the younger brother who saw his sin and confessed it?

✛ Read Psalm 103:8–14. What does this say about God? What does this say about us? What condition do you see for God's love and forgiveness in verse 11? What does it mean to "fear God"?

✛ Write out 1 John 1:9, Isaiah 43:25, and Psalm 103:12 on an index card and put it in your "God's Promises" box. Using these verses to help you pray, thank God for His promise of forgiveness. What sins do you need to confess?

✛ *Activity:* Get rid of some garbage! Weed a garden; clean out a box of markers, a drawer, or closet. As you do this, remember that we must look for the sin in our hearts and get rid of it through true confession. With God's help, turn from sin. After all, it would be foolish to put the garbage back after you cleaned it out.

With You Always and Everywhere

When you were little, what were you afraid to do? What helped you to do it?

Maybe you were afraid to go down the slide. But if your dad said, "I will catch you at the bottom," it was easier to do. It made you brave to know that someone else was there—watching and helping if you needed it.

Or maybe you had to get a shot at the doctor's office. No one likes that. But if your mother said, "I will hold your hand," it wasn't as hard to do.

How about going down into a dark basement by yourself—that can be kind of scary! But if your brother or sister offers to go with you, it is not quite as scary. You are a little braver if you know someone is with you. The basement is just as dark, but you are not alone.

It makes us feel better to have someone with us. Just knowing that another person is with us and that we are not alone is a comfort to us.

After Moses died, Joshua had a hard job to do. But he wasn't facing it alone. God promised to be with him:

Just as I was with Moses, so I will be with you. I will not leave you or forsake you. (Joshua 1:5)

Joshua's hard job was to lead the people of Israel across the Jordan River into the land that God had promised them. That land was filled with many people who did not like the Israelites and would fight with them.

It would be scary for Joshua to lead all those battles for the land by himself. But he wasn't alone. This is what God promised him:

Have I not commanded you? Be strong and courageous. Do not be frightened, and do not be dismayed, for the LORD your God is with you wherever you go. (Joshua 1:9)

God gave Joshua a job to do. God commanded Joshua to take the land. But God did not leave Joshua alone. God went with him and helped him. He promised never to leave Joshua. Knowing that God was with him and would help him was a great comfort to Joshua.

Having someone with you is a good thing, but having God with you is a GREAT thing! He is bigger and stronger than anything we face. He understands our fears and is ready to help if we ask.

People can't be with us everywhere all the time. And there are many things that are bigger and stronger than people. But nothing is stronger than God. And He is with us all the time, everywhere. He is never on vacation. He never sleeps, and He is always paying attention.

Can you get away from the air in this room without leaving the room? No, that is silly, isn't it? As long as you are in this room, you are surrounded by air. You can't get away from it.

Just like the air fills the room and you can't get away from it, so you can't get away from God. Do you know why? This verse tells us why:

Can a man hide himself in secret places so that I cannot see him? declares the Lord. Do I not fill heaven and earth? declares the Lord. (Jeremiah 23:24)

No one can hide from God because God is everywhere, all the time—He fills heaven and earth. God is in every place, every state, every house, and every room—always. He is with you right now.

This is a scary thought for people who are evil and want to hide the evil things they do from God. But if you love God, this is a comforting thought. No matter where you go or what you are doing, God is right there with you. He gives courage to His people when things are scary, comfort when they are sad, and help when they are weak. And this promise is *forever!*

Always God is with us. Every moment of every day. This is the wonderful promise Jesus made to His disciples and to all those who trust and love Him:

And behold, I am with you always, to the end of the age. (Matthew 28:20)

Does this promise fill you with joy and comfort, or is it scary that you cannot hide from God?

LEARNING TO TRUST GOD

✦ Read Joshua 1:1–9. What promises did God make? What did God tell Joshua to do? Read Joshua 21:43–45. What does this tell you about God?

✦ Write out Joshua 1:9 and Matthew 28:20 on an index card and put it in your "God's Promises" box. Think of some of the times and places where God was with you today. Is this a comfort or a worry to you?

✦ *Activity:* Discover some "hidden" things. Go for a walk in the woods. Look under rocks and bushes to see what you can find. Although those things were hidden from you, remember that nothing is hidden from God. Give praise to God who is everywhere all the time, who knows every part of His creation at all times, and who promises to always be with His people.

Steadfast Love

Do you know what "from everlasting to everlasting" means? It means that it never comes to an end. Most things come to an end—summer vacation, an ice cream cone, a good book, and all kinds of other things. But the Bible tells us a promise about something that never ends—something that is from everlasting to everlasting:

> But the steadfast love of the Lord is from everlasting to everlasting on those who fear him. (Psalm 103:17)

God's love is forever—it never ends! It goes on and on and on. Nothing can stop it. It is from everlasting to everlasting.

You probably already noticed that this is not a promise for everyone. Who is this promise for? It is for those who "fear" God—for His children who respect, love, and obey Him.

God will never stop loving His people. He will never stop being their God—no matter what. Peter found that out. The steadfast, never-ending love of Jesus never left Peter.

After Jesus was arrested in the garden of Gethsemane, Peter followed Jesus and His arrestors to the house of the high priest. But Peter didn't follow very closely because he was afraid. He was so afraid that when a servant girl recognized him as someone who was with Jesus, "he denied it, saying, "Woman, I do not know him" (Luke 22:57).

Peter was more afraid for himself than he was loyal to Jesus. He denied Jesus, not just once but three times. After the third time, Jesus just looked at him.

Jesus was disappointed in Peter. It made Him sad that Peter would say that he didn't even know Him. Peter knew that he had sinned very deeply and that he had not shown steadfast love to Jesus. So he "wept bitterly."

But that was not the end for Peter. Jesus does not stop loving His children—even when they disappoint Him. He loves them from everlasting to everlasting. Jesus showed Peter His steadfast love after He rose from the dead.

Jesus was on the beach when the disciples returned from fishing. He made them a fish breakfast and, after they ate, Jesus asked Peter whether he loved

Him. Three times He asked Peter, and three times Peter said, "Yes." Earlier, Peter had denied Jesus three times. Now he declared his love for Jesus three times.

Jesus forgave Peter. With tender love, He gave Peter a new job—to teach people about Him. Jesus did not stop loving Peter or stop being his friend . . . because His love is from everlasting to everlasting . . . no matter what.

Nothing can take away God's love—nothing at all, anywhere, anytime:

For I am sure that neither death nor life, nor angels nor rulers, nor things present nor things to come, nor powers, nor height nor depth, nor anything else in all creation, will be able to separate us from the love of God in Christ Jesus our Lord. (Romans 8:38–39)

Peter learned that nothing can take away God's love. But he would not turn away from God the next time he was asked! When he was told not to teach about Jesus, Peter stood firm and spoke out. He said, "No"—he had to speak about Jesus. He would obey God and stand against the men who wanted him to stop talking about Jesus.[1]

God's steadfast love never left Peter. It changed him from being a scared Jesus-denier to a bold Jesus-preacher. If you are trusting in Jesus, then God's steadfast love will never leave you either, and God's work in your life will never end. He will make you strong like Peter.

And I am sure of this, that he who began a good work in you will bring it to completion at the day of Jesus Christ. (Philippians 1:6)

1. Acts 4:1–22

LEARNING TO TRUST GOD

✤ Read Romans 8:35–39. Look at the long list of things that cannot separate God's children from Him. Then make your own list of things in your life that cannot separate you from God if you are His child.

✤ Write out Psalm 103:17, Romans 8:38–39, and Philippians 1:6 on an index card and put it in your "God's Promises" box. Thank God for His steadfast love.

✤ *Activity:* Find out how penguins take care of their eggs, or watch the clip about penguins in the movie titled *Planet Earth*.[2] How are these penguins a reflection of their Creator?

2. *Planet Earth*. Episode 1, "From Pole to Pole." Narrated by David Attenborough and Sigourney Weaver. BBC Warner, 2007. Film.

Ears That Hear

God kept His promise to Abraham and made from him the great nation of Israel. He brought the Israelites out of slavery in Egypt and gave them food and water in the wilderness. He defeated their enemies in Canaan and kept all the promises He gave Israel through Joshua.

Even so, Israel wasn't sure about God. Was He really God . . . or was the idol, Baal, god? Which one should they follow?

But Elijah the prophet was sure. The God of Israel is the one true God, and Elijah would follow Him.

> And Elijah came near to all the people and said, "How long will you go limping between two different opinions? If the LORD is God, follow him; but if Baal, then follow him." And the people did not answer him a word. (1 Kings 18:21)

So Elijah suggested a test. The 450 prophets of Baal would pile up some wood, and cut up a bull to lay in pieces on top of the wood. Elijah would do the same. What was the test Elijah suggested?

> And you call upon the name of your god, and I will call upon the name of the LORD, and the God who answers by fire, he is God. (1 Kings 18:24)

The prophets of Baal called out to their god all morning, but an answer never came.

What do you do when someone doesn't hear you? Maybe you talk louder . . . or do something else to get the person's attention?

That's just what the 450 prophets of Baal did. They **"cried aloud."** And then they did something really strange to get Baal's attention—**"they . . . cut themselves . . .**

with swords and lances, until the blood gushed out upon them" (1 Kings 18:28). Surely that would get the attention of a god!

But "No one answered; no one paid attention" (1 Kings 18:29). Praying to Baal was useless, because he was an idol and not the one true God. The prophets of Baal didn't understand:

> Their idols are silver and gold,
> > the work of human hands.
> They have mouths, but do not speak;
> > eyes, but do not see.
> They have ears, but do not hear;
> > noses, but do not smell. (Psalm 115:4–6)

Then it was Elijah's turn . . . his turn to show the people who is the one true God and what He is like. Do you know what Elijah did? He soaked the wood with water, so it would be hard to burn. Then he prayed:

"O Lord, God of Abraham, Isaac, and Israel, let it be known this day that you are God in Israel, and that I am your servant, and that I have done all these things at your word. Answer me, O Lord, answer me, that this people may know that you,

O Lord, are God, and that you have turned their hearts back." Then the fire of the Lord fell and consumed the burnt offering and the wood and the stones and the dust, and licked up the water that was in the trench. And when all the people saw it, they fell on their faces and said, "The Lord, he is God; the Lord, he is God." (1 Kings 18:36–39)

God is not like the false idols that can't see or hear. God is the one true God. He is real and living. He sees everything and everyone. He hears all things—even the tiniest whisper. And best of all:

> The eyes of the Lord are toward the righteous
>   and his ears toward their cry. (Psalm 34:15)

God is always watching, always listening to His people. He hears every time they pray. And He answers every prayer.

If you are a Christian, God hears all your prayers—every one of them. And He answers every one—even when it doesn't seem like it. Just like any polite person, God answers when you call on Him.

Sometimes His answer is "yes," like when He answered Hannah's prayer for a baby and gave her Samuel. Sometimes His answer is "no," because He knows what we really need better than we do. And sometimes His answer is "wait," because the time is not right. Sometimes the answer is on the way, but we don't know it because we can't see what God is doing.

God's promise to His people is that He will hear and answer every prayer they pray.

> For you, O Lord, are good and forgiving,
>   abounding in steadfast love to all who call upon you.
> Give ear, O Lord, to my prayer;
>   listen to my plea for grace.

In the day of my trouble I call upon you,
for you answer me.

There is none like you among the gods, O Lord,
nor are there any works like yours. (Psalm 86:5–8)

LEARNING TO TRUST GOD

✤ Read the story of Elijah and the fire of God in 1 Kings 18:17–40. What does it mean to go "limping between two opinions"? What does standing firm in faith in God look like in your life? Do you follow God alone, or do you limp between two opinions?

✤ Write out Psalm 34:15 on an index card and put it in your "God's Promises" box. With your family, split up the cards in the box and then pray using the cards. Thank God for His wonderful promises.

✤ *Activity:* Attend a prayer gathering with your family. Remember that God always hears us when we pray.

Every Need Supplied

How much food do you think a bird eats in a day? There is no one answer because it depends on the size of the bird, the season of the year, the temperature of the air, and other things. But a bird can eat as much as half its body weight in one day. And a hummingbird can swallow as much sugar water and flower nectar as its full body weight . . . and eat as many as 2,000 tiny bugs . . . in one day![1] That is a lot of bugs in one day! Where do they get all those bugs?

God feeds the birds . . . every day. He cares for birds and other animals . . . and even flowers, giving them beautiful petals to wear.

Jesus said,

Look at the birds of the air: they neither sow nor reap nor gather into barns, and yet your heavenly Father feeds them. Are you not of more value than they? (Matthew 6:26)

What did Jesus mean when he said, "Are you not of more value than they?" If God cares for birds, which are not nearly as important as people, then He will surely care for His very own people!

Do you remember how He cared for Israel in the wilderness, where there was no food or water? The Israelites were worried . . . and scared. Where would they get food and water? They foolishly thought it would have been better to stay in Egypt as slaves.

But God had His own way of caring for them. He made bad-tasting water sweet, and He opened a rock to pour out water.[2] He sent birds called "quail" to

1. The Cornell Lab of Ornithology, *All About Birds*, accessed 8/11/11; http://www.allaboutbirds.org/page.aspx?pid=1277.
2. Exodus 15:23–25; 17:6

feed them. He rained down from heaven special bread called manna. For 40 years—the whole time Israel was in the wilderness, God gave them the special manna bread.[3] They always had food to eat. And they always had water to drink.

3. Exodus 16:35

Jesus said that God's children do not need to worry about food or clothes . . . or about anything, because God knows what we need. He tells us to do what is most important—to love and obey God, and to show others how to love God.

But seek first the kingdom of God and his righteousness, and all these things will be added to you. (Matthew 6:33)

God will give His children everything they need, but they must make following Jesus the most important thing in their lives. It must be more important than playing a game, doing homework, or eating breakfast. It must be more important than clothes, food, money . . . or anything.

Following Jesus was most important to Paul, even though it meant being thrown into prison for preaching about God. The jails in those days were not like jails today, where the prisoners are given meals every day. Sometimes the people didn't eat unless friends brought them food. How would God care for Paul in prison?

God made people of the church in Philippi willing and able to help Paul. So the church sent a man named Epaphroditus to Paul with gifts—food and other things. Paul was very grateful to the church in Philippi, but he was mostly grateful to God, who was the true Giver of the gifts.

Would the church now have what it needed? Paul was not worried about what the church in Philippi needed. He knew that God takes care of His children, and he told them:

And my God will supply every need of yours according to his riches in glory in Christ Jesus. (Philippians 4:19)

If you are a Christian, God has already taken care of your greatest need—forgiveness for sin through Jesus' death on the cross. But He has promised to care for other needs, too—"all these things will be added to you." Do you love God most of all? Is it most important to you to follow Him?

But seek first the kingdom of God and his righteousness, and all these things will be added to you. (Matthew 6:33)

LEARNING TO TRUST GOD

✢ Read Exodus 16 and see how God cared for His children in the wilderness. How did God show His goodness and faithfulness to them?

✢ Write out Matthew 6:33 and Philippians 4:19 on an index card and put it in your "God's Promises" box. Ask your mother or father to tell you about a time when God provided for them in a special way.

✢ *Activity:* Just as God cared for Paul through the gifts of the Philippian church, so God cares for people today through the gifts of Christians. What needs do you see in your neighborhood or church, or in the world? What gift can your family give to be part of God's caring work for others? Ask God to show you what you can do and then do it.

No Good Thing Withheld

Why would someone not give you a gift that would be good for you?
  Did you think of these reasons?

- He is selfish—he wants to keep it for himself.
- He doesn't have it.
- He doesn't know that you want it.
- He doesn't like you.

Which of these reasons is true of God?

  None of them! God is not selfish; He is generous. When Jesus fed the 5,000, He gave them more than enough fish and bread to eat. He gave them so much that there were 12 baskets of food left over.

  There is nothing God does not have. He owns the whole world and everything in it. He knows what you want because He knows everything. And we know that God isn't unloving, because the Bible says that "God is love" (1 John 4:18). So if there is something that is good for His children, God will give it to them. We know this is true because God has made a never-ending promise about this:

> For the LORD God is a sun and shield;
>   the LORD bestows favor and honor.
> No good thing does he withhold
>   from those who walk uprightly. (Psalm 84:11)

Who is this promise for? Who are "those who walk uprightly"?

Those who walk uprightly are those who trust and love God and follow His ways. So, for the Christian who loves and obeys God, God does not withhold—hold back—even one thing that is good for him.

Does God only give small things, but hold back on the really big things? It is easy to give away things that don't matter to us. It's much harder to give things we really like or that cost us a lot of money.

What do you think would be the biggest, most important thing for God to give? God gave to His people His very own Son. Jesus left His home in heaven, came to earth, and died on a cross. God has given the greatest and the best! So does He withhold things that are less important or precious?

He who did not spare his own Son but gave him up for us all, how will he not also with him graciously give us all things? (Romans 8:32)

Since God gave the very best already, His most precious Son, He will give His children *everything* that is good for them. He will not withhold even one little thing. If there is something God does not give to a believer in Jesus, it is because that thing is not good for him or is not right for him at that time.

A little girl named Amy Carmichael really wanted blue eyes instead of brown. She prayed many times, asking God to give her blue eyes. But God did not give her blue eyes—He withheld them from her.

Amy grew up with her brown eyes and became a missionary to India. And guess what color eyes the people in India had? Brown eyes! Brown-eyed Amy fit in very well with the brown-eyed people of India. A blue-eyed Amy would not have fit in as well.

God knew that Amy Carmichael would grow up to be a missionary in India and that brown eyes were better for her. When Amy was grown up, she knew that brown eyes were better for her. God had not withheld something good from her.

It takes faith to trust when God does not give us something we ask for, because it is not good for us. Do you believe that God is generous, all-powerful, all-knowing, and loving? Do you believe God's promise to His children?

The young lions suffer want and hunger;
    but those who seek the LORD lack no good thing. (Psalm 34:10)

LEARNING TO TRUST GOD

✦ Read Psalm 34. Does God's promise not to withhold anything good mean that nothing bad will ever happen to a Christian? How can something bad actually be good? What does "good" mean?[1]

✦ Write out Psalm 84:10 and Psalm 34:10 on an index card and put it in your "God's Promises" box. With your family, make a list of some of the good things God has not withheld from your family. In what ways were these things good?

✦ *Activity:* God is very generous and loves it when people follow His ways. In what way can you or your family be generous to someone else?

---

1. Parents: Make sure that your child understands that "good" means what is ultimately beneficial for us, and that sometimes suffering and hardship can be good for us to teach us to depend on God, to sanctify us, etc. The greater good that God has for His children is that they be "conformed to the image of his son" (Romans 8:29).

A Present Help

The people of Israel were hiding in caves. Why were they doing this? The Israelites disobeyed God over and over, so God did something to cause Israel to turn back to Him. He sent their enemies, the Midianites. That is why the Israelites were hiding in caves.[1] They were scared . . . very scared.

Do you know how the Bible describes the Midianites? It says they were like locusts (grasshoppers). Locusts can swarm over a farmer's field, and in just a few hours they can devour everything, leaving nothing for the farmer.

This is just what the Midianites did. They swarmed over the land of Israel and stole all the crops growing in the fields, all the sheep, oxen, and donkeys . . . and left nothing for the Israelites. For seven years, the devouring Midianites came like swarms of locusts.

And the people of Israel cried out for help to the Lord. (Judges 6:6)

When things got bad, Israel knew where to turn—to God Almighty, the One they had turned away from. God loves to forgive those who turn away from sin, and He hears the prayers of His people, so He answered the Israelites. He chose Gideon to lead some men to fight the Midianites.

Gideon was very nervous about this plan. How would fearful Gideon and the fearful Israelites hiding in caves fight the Midianites?

They would not fight alone. Their great and mighty God said,

But I will be with you. (Judges 6:16)

1. Judges 6:1–2

God, who is always with His people, doesn't just sit back and watch what is going on with His people. He works for them. He fights for them. He helps them.

> God is our refuge and strength,
>   a very present help in trouble. (Psalm 46:1)

Israel was surely in a time of trouble! But this trouble was no problem for the God of the Universe, who made all things and holds all things together. The swarming, devouring Midianites could not stand against the power of God.

Gideon gathered a big army of men. But God didn't need a big army. In fact, He doesn't need an army at all. But He used a little army of only 300 men . . . and trumpets, torches, and empty jars. What would God do with such strange "weapons"?

The Israelites sneaked down and surrounded the camp of the Midianites with a trumpet in one hand and a torch covered by a jar in the other hand. When Gideon blew his trumpet, all the men blew their trumpets, broke the jars, and shouted:

A sword for the Lord and for Gideon! (Judges 7:20)

What did God, the "very present help in trouble," do?

The Lord set every man's sword against his comrade and against all the army. (Judges 7:22)

The devouring Midianites were now like the fearful Israelites! They were so scared and confused that they started fighting with themselves! Then they ran away!

Have you ever heard of such a strange battle and such a great victory! Only the Lord could work for His people in such a way. No one is like the Lord God!

From of old no one has heard
    or perceived by the ear,
no eye has seen a God besides you,
    who acts for those who wait for him. (Isaiah 64:4)

If you are a Christian, God is your very present Helper, too. When you are sad, scared, or have problems, He is always ready to help and fight for you. When you arc tempted to sin or to doubt the Bible, He will fight for your faith. He is a God who *acts*. He doesn't just sit and watch. He is not far off, or uninterested in your life. He is *very present*, and He *acts* for His people.

Do you have any problems, fears, or worries today? Have you asked God for His help, or are you struggling alone?

LEARNING TO TRUST GOD

✣ Read about how God helped Israel in Judges 7. What does this story tell you about God? How did God help you and your family this week?

✣ Write out Psalm 46:1 and Isaiah 64:4 on an index card. What does "refuge" mean? How can God be your strength? What condition is given in Isaiah 64:4? What does it mean to "wait for him"? Pray using your verses, and then put the card in your "God's Promises" box.

✣ *Activity:* The Bible tells us to remember the goodness of the Lord. Ask your parents to tell you about some unusual times when God helped them or your family. Write down, illustrate, or make a video of one of these stories of God's help. Then share the story with someone to encourage his faith.

Strength in Weakness

Have you ever been nervous about having to ask a stranger a question? Or about giving an answer in class—speaking in front of everyone in the room?

Moses was nervous, too. He had to ask Pharaoh, the king of Egypt, to free the Hebrew people Pharaoh used as slaves. Moses didn't want to talk to Pharaoh. He was scared. So he told God that he didn't speak very well.

Do you remember what God did? God, the Maker of all things—like mouths and speaking—said He would help Moses. But Moses was still scared, and he asked God to send someone else. God did not send someone instead of Moses. God sent someone to help Moses, his brother Aaron.[1] What does this tell you about God?

God is understanding of our weakness. He doesn't make fun of us for being weak or scared. Instead, He offers His help and His strength.

> Have you not known? Have you not heard?
> The Lord is the everlasting God,
>   the Creator of the ends of the earth.
> He does not faint or grow weary;
>   his understanding is unsearchable.
> He gives power to the faint,
>   and to him who has no might he increases strength. (Isaiah 40:28–29)

Someone else was very scared to speak, too. Whenever he had to speak in class as a child, he would get choked up. He could only give very short answers when

---

1. Exodus 4:10–17

the teacher called on him. His hands shook when he had to do math problems on the board. It was very embarrassing.[2] Have you ever had this problem?

His problem with being very nervous didn't end when he got to high school. But the biggest problem came when he had to give a speech in front of his Spanish class. A speech is more than a few words. It is a lot of sentences. How could he do it? What advice would you give him?

Because he was a Christian, this person knew where to turn. He turned to God, who is a "very present help in trouble." He prayed and prayed, asking God

2. John Piper, *Future Grace* (Sisters, OR: Multnomah, 1995), 51.

to help him. And he reminded himself of God's promises. What promise would you remind him of?

When the day of the speech came, he was shaking. It wasn't the best speech . . . but he got through it! God gave him the strength to face the class, open his mouth, and speak!

When we admit that we are weak and depend on God, He gives us His strength to help us. God is so eager to strengthen and help us that He actually looks for those who need help. Can you believe that God is actually *eager* to make us strong? This is what the Bible says:

> For the eyes of the LORD run to and fro throughout the whole earth, to give strong support to those whose heart is blameless toward him.
> (2 Chronicles 16:9)

God gives His children strength to do things that are hard for them to do—like talk in front of the class, do their school work, go through sickness, and be kind to someone who is mean. When we trust God with the hard things in our lives, He gives us the strength to go through them.

Have you ever seen a flimsy vine—like a tomato or ivy vine? They can't stand up on their own. So vines cling to other things for support. A tomato plant can grow on a fence or a pole. Ivy sometimes climbs up strong trees or even the side of a building. The strong fence, tree, or building holds or supports the vine.

That is what it is like when we "cling" to Jesus. He helps us to be strong, because He is strong. That is what the boy who was afraid to talk in front of the class did. He trusted in Jesus, and Jesus supported him and made him strong.

Do you know what happened to the boy? God gave him strength and courage . . . and he became a famous *preacher who speaks in front of thousands of people!* His name is John Piper, and he preaches a lot, showing that this promise is really true for those who trust God:

My grace is sufficient for you, for my power is made perfect in weakness. (2 Corinthians 12:9)

In what way are you weak? What is hard for you? You can use your own strength—and that is all you will have. Or you can "cling" to Jesus, trusting Him to make you strong and give you His strength.

LEARNING TO TRUST GOD

✤ Read 2 Corinthians 12:7–10. What was God's answer to Paul's prayer? How could Paul be strong when he was weak?

✤ Write out Isaiah 40:28–29, 2 Chronicles 16:9, and 2 Corinthians 12:9 on an index card, and put it in your "God's Promises" box. Thank God that He gives strength to those who trust in Him. This week, do something that is hard for you. You will either do it with your own strength, or depend on God for His strength.

✤ *Activity:* Plant a tomato plant or a vine. When it grows, you will be able to see its weakness. Use something to support it and remind yourself that we, too, need to depend on God to make us strong.

Slow to Anger

Can you imagine being upset because someone was patient instead of quick to become angry? That's what happened with a prophet God sent to preach to the people of Nineveh. Do you know who that prophet was? It was Jonah. Do you know who Jonah was upset with? He was upset with God!

This is what Jonah knew about God:[1]

> But you, O Lord, are a God merciful and gracious,
>   slow to anger and abounding in steadfast love and faithfulness.
>   (Psalm 86:15)

This made Jonah quite upset. Nineveh was an important city, but it was also a place of much evil. The people of Nineveh deserved God's anger and punishment. But God had compassion for Nineveh. He wanted Jonah to preach to the people of Nineveh—to tell them to turn away from their evil ways. He wanted to give them another chance so they would not be destroyed.

But Jonah didn't feel this way. He wanted God to destroy Nineveh. So he ran away on a ship—as if anyone can run from God, who is everywhere all the time! But God didn't let Jonah run away. What happened with the storm at sea and the great fish?[2]

After the fish spit up Jonah, God told Jonah a second time to preach to Nineveh. This time Jonah obeyed. But he wasn't very happy about it. Do you know what that feels like?

Jonah preached in Nineveh and warned the people that if they did not repent—turn from their sins—God would destroy them in 40 days. God, who is "merciful

1. In Jonah 4:2, Jonah repeats this promise. Psalm 86:15 is used in the story because it is a more concise verse to memorize.
2. If your child is not familiar with the story, stop and tell him the story from Jonah 1–2.

and gracious" and "slow to anger," gave the people of Nineveh hearts of repentance. They were truly sorry for their sin.

The king of Nineveh even ordered his people to stop eating, to dress in sad-looking clothes, and to ask God not to destroy them. The king told them to turn from their evil ways and from hurting each other.

When God saw their sorrow over sin and that they wanted to turn away from evil, He acted just as He has promised:

The LORD is merciful and gracious,
    slow to anger and abounding in steadfast love.
He will not always chide,
    nor will he keep his anger forever.
He does not deal with us according to our sins,
    nor repay us according to our iniquities. (Psalm 103:8–10)

The writer of this psalm is telling us what God is like, and what He promises to be. God promises to be patient—not to get angry quickly, but to be slow to anger. He promises to treat us better . . . much better than we deserve.

God did not treat the people of Nineveh as they deserved to be treated. They were not punished for their great sins. God was merciful and gracious, and He promised not to destroy Nineveh. He showed them kindness instead of anger.

How do you think Jonah felt about this? He was angry. He knew God would be merciful and gracious instead of getting angry and destroying Nineveh. That is why he didn't want to preach in Nineveh. He wanted them punished. He was so angry that he said he wanted to die. Then Jonah sat under a shade plant to pout . . . until a worm ate the plant, and Jonah was angry about that, too. He was not at all like God, who is slow to anger.

God could have been very angry with Jonah. He could have told Jonah that he could not be a prophet anymore. Or He could have let Jonah drown in the sea when he tried to run away. God could have destroyed Jonah for having such a bad attitude and not repenting from it. But He didn't. Why not?

As a father shows compassion to his children,
    so the LORD shows compassion to those who fear him.
For he knows our frame;
    he remembers that we are dust. (Psalm 103:13–14)

God understands that man was made from the dust of the earth.[3] He knows that we are weak and find it hard to turn from sin. He is patient with us. He wants to help us, not destroy us.

God was slow to anger and did not destroy Nineveh. He was also patient with angry Jonah. Even though Jonah did not act like someone who fears God, Jonah was a prophet who did trust God. So God showed Him great compassion in being slow to anger.

If God was slow to anger with evil Nineveh, how much more patient do you think He will be with His children? If you are trusting in Jesus and want to turn from sin and follow Him, God's promise to be slow to anger is for you, too. This should fill you with great joy, because we need God's patience very much. Why do you need God's patience?

3. Genesis 2:7

LEARNING TO TRUST GOD

✤ Read Psalm 103:8–14. Look up any words you do not know. Then explain the verses to your father or mother.

✤ Write out Psalm 86:15 and 103:8–10 on an index card, and put it in your "God's Promises" box. What are some times when God has been slow to anger with you? Are you patient with others? Thank God for His slowness to anger, and ask Him to give you a patient heart.

✤ *Activity:* God is slow to anger because He has great compassion. When we show compassion, He is pleased. Think of a family your family could bless. It could be a family having a hard time, who aren't Christians, or any family. Maybe you could bring them a meal, invite them for dinner, babysit the children, fix something for them, or do some yard work. Ask God for an idea, and bless them!

Discipline, a Gift?

Do you remember the story of Jonah? Why could we call Jonah "the angry prophet"? What wrong things did Jonah do because of his angry heart? Here are some examples:

- He disobeyed God by getting on a ship going away from Nineveh.
- He did not have compassion for the people of Nineveh and was angry at God for not destroying Nineveh.
- He wanted to die, and He pouted.
- He was not trusting God's wisdom, justice, and right to rule the world.

Is God so loving, forgiving, and slow to anger that Jonah's sin didn't matter? Did God do anything about this?

Although God is slow to anger, He did not ignore Jonah's sin. What did He do when Jonah sailed away from Nineveh?

God sent a storm that almost caused the boat to overturn, so the sailors threw Jonah into the sea. God could have let Jonah drown for being so disobedient. But He didn't. God is full of compassion, so He sent a big fish to swallow Jonah. But Jonah had to be in the belly of the fish for three days. What do you think that was like?

When the fish spit up Jonah, Jonah was ready to obey God. God disciplined Jonah to turn him away from his disobedience. Jonah probably did not like being in the belly of the big fish, but he needed to be stopped in his sin. So God, in love, stopped him.

God did the same thing for King David. David sinned by taking another man's wife and then having her husband killed. This was a great evil. But David sinned even more by hiding his sin. He did not confess his sin to God. Do you think God let David stay in his sin? What would it be like for David to have to hide that sin every day, knowing in his heart that it was there?

God loved David so much with His never-ending steadfast love that He would not let David keep on sinning by hiding his sin. So He sent Nathan, a prophet, to show David his sin and to let him know that no sin is really hidden. God wanted David to be free from his sin and to have a clean heart.

When Nathan told David about his sin, David did not pretend he had not sinned. He didn't make excuses, and he didn't get angry. He admitted his sin:

David said to Nathan, "I have sinned against the LORD." And Nathan said to David, "The LORD also has put away your sin; you shall not die." (2 Samuel 12:13)

When David confessed his sin, God was "faithful and just to forgive" his sin. But there was a consequence for David's sin. There would be trouble in David's home, and the baby that would be born to David and his wife would not live.

Do you think God did this to be mean? Can you think of a time when you were disciplined for something? Why were you disciplined?

Just as your parents show you your wrongdoings and your sinful heart, and then give you consequences because they love you, so God disciplines His children because He loves them. He does not want them to keep sinning or to have sin in their hearts.

Your mother and father would not be very good parents if they did not discipline you. And God would not be a good Father to His children if He did not discipline them. But He is a good Father, and He has even made a promise to discipline His children.

It is a wonderful gift that God acts to keep His children from continuing in their sin. It might not seem like a gift, but it really is. To keep on sinning would bring us deeper and deeper into bad living and sinful attitudes. God loves His children too much to let that happen. We should be very grateful for God's wonderful promise to discipline. The Bible tells us:

My son, do not despise the LORD's discipline
  or be weary of his reproof,
for the LORD reproves him whom he loves,
  as a father the son in whom he delights. (Proverbs 3:11–12)

Do you know what "despise" means? It means "to hate." We should not get angry when God disciplines us through our parents or teachers, or through consequences. He is loving us.

When you are disciplined, are you grateful, or are you angry? Do you admit when you are wrong, like David did?

For the moment all discipline seems painful rather than pleasant, but later it yields the peaceful fruit of righteousness to those who have been trained by it. (Hebrews 12:11)

LEARNING TO TRUST GOD

✣ Read Hebrews 12:5–11. Explain it in your own words. Share with your mom or dad about a time when you were disciplined and how that has helped you.

✣ Write out Proverbs 3:11–12 on an index card and put it in your "God's Promises" box. Look up the words you don't know. Talk with your mother or father about how you handle discipline. Thank God for His promise to discipline His children.

✣ *Activity:* Make a nice poster of the Ten Commandments for your home. Talk about why God's commands are good, and why it is good when we are disciplined for disobeying them.

Everything for Good

Suppose you woke up on your birthday to find a big box in your room. Inside you heard some scratching noises. What might be in the box?

Suppose in this box there was a cute, brown, wiggly puppy. Would you be excited? What kinds of plans might you make for this little puppy?

Maybe you would give it a name and teach it some tricks. Maybe you would plan to buy a collar and a toy for the puppy or to build it a doghouse. You could plan all kinds of good things.

Would you plan to leave the puppy out in the cold, or to let it go hungry? Or to let it run into the street where it might be hit by a car? Of course not. Your plans for the puppy would be for good.

Are you as good, smart, and loving as God? No, but still you would plan good things, not bad, for your puppy. If you would plan good for your puppy, wouldn't God so much more plan good for His own children? Of course! God even said so in this promise to Israel and to all who are adopted into Abraham's family by faith in Jesus:

> For I know the plans I have for you, declares the LORD, plans for welfare and not for evil, to give you a future and a hope. (Jeremiah 29:11)

If God is in charge of all things,[1] and His plans for His children are for good, then everything that happens to a child of God is for his good.

Everything? Even a disease like leprosy? Leprosy is a really bad disease that can give people bad scabs and sores. Sometimes they lose the feeling in their feet or hands and become paralyzed so they can't move parts of their bodies. How could leprosy work for good?

1. Ephesians 1:11

Naaman was an important army commander in Syria in Bible times. He didn't love or serve God, but his wife had a girl from Israel as her maid. The maid knew about Elisha, the prophet, and she believed that God would cure Naaman's leprosy. So Naaman went to see Elisha.

When Naaman got to Elisha's house, Elisha sent a messenger to Naaman to tell him to wash in the Jordan River seven times. This made Naaman angry. He thought Elisha himself would come out to see him, call on God, wave his hand around, and cure the leprosy. After all, Naaman was an important commander. . . . Anyway, he thought, weren't the rivers of Syria better than the rivers of Israel?

But Naaman's servants convinced him to follow Elisha's instructions. So Naaman went and dipped in the Jordan River seven times, just as Elisha had said . . . and Naaman was healed! The leprosy was gone!

But the best part of this true story is that Naaman went back to Elisha's house and said:

Behold, I know that there is no God in all the earth but in Israel. (2 Kings 5:15)

God used leprosy to give Naaman the best gift of all—faith in the God of Israel as the one true God. Naaman didn't honor God at first, but God worked all things, including leprosy, so that Naaman would know and honor God. So the bad disease, leprosy, was used for good in Naaman's life.

Romans 8:28 says:

> And we know that for those who love God all things work together for good, for those who are called according to his purpose.

For those who love God, all things work for good—not just two or three things, not just some things, not even just most things, but all things. Every single thing that happens to a Christian is given by God for that person's good. This means we can be sure that everything—sunny days and rainy days, happy times and hard times, having to talk in front of the class or do homework, disappointing news and good news, having a lot of money or having little money . . . all things . . . every single thing will work for our good if we love God most of all.

We don't need to worry about anything in our lives or be afraid of what might happen, because God's promise to His children is that every single thing—big or little—will, in the end, be good for the person who loves God.

This is a wonderful promise! A great promise! From a great and loving God!

> The steadfast love of the LORD never ceases;
>> his mercies never come to an end;
> they are new every morning;
>> great is your faithfulness. (Lamentations 3:22–23)

LEARNING TO TRUST GOD

✤ Read Romans 8:28 again. What does "good" mean? Is it the same as "pleasant"? Think of some of the things that happened to you this week. How could they work out for your good? This is a wonderful promise, but remember that this promise is for "those who love God." If you are not a Christian, why is that very bad news? If you are a Christian, is there anything in your life you need to trust God to work for your good?

✤ Write out Jeremiah 29:11, Romans 8:28, and Lamentations 3:22–23 on an index card and put it in your "God's Promises" box. With your family, make a list of God's mercies to your family today. Then thank God for those mercies.

✤ *Activity:* Read Psalm 112:6–7. Why can the righteous, those who are trusting in Jesus, be unafraid of bad news? Sometimes our faith is weak and we need someone to remind us that God's promise in Romans 8:28 is true. Is there someone your family can encourage this week who might need this reminder? Make them a card, pray for them, visit them with your promise box and remind them of God's promises, or encourage them in another way.

No Unnecessary Suffering

When you scrape your knee, how do adults take care of it? Usually, they clean it with soap and water, and maybe spray some medication on it. Does that hurt? Yes, in taking care of your scrape, they often make it hurt more.

If that makes it hurt more, why do they do it? They do it to keep you from getting an infection—which *really* hurts and can make you very sick. The short pain they give you in the moment keeps you from greater pain and bigger problems later on.

God "cleans our scraped knees," too—He does what He needs to do to keep His children from worse problems later. He has promised not to bring more suffering than necessary into the lives of Christians:

> But, though he cause grief, he will have compassion
>   according to the abundance of his steadfast love;
> for he does not willingly afflict
>   or grieve the children of men. (Lamentations 3:32–33)

Because God is kind and loves with a never-ending love, He does not like to bring pain, sadness, or suffering to people. But He does what He must for our good.

Jesus had a very good friend named Lazarus. Lazarus got very sick. So his sisters, Mary and Martha, asked Jesus to come to them. Jesus loved Lazarus and his sisters very much, but Jesus did not go to help them. He let Lazarus die. Doesn't this seem strange? Why would He do this? Jesus went to them *after* Lazarus died. Jesus could have gone earlier and healed Lazarus . . . but He didn't.

When Jesus came and saw Mary and her friends crying, Jesus cried, too. It made Him sad to see how sad they were. But more than that, He was sad that they did not have faith in Him and in God's goodness and greatness.

Jesus went to the tomb where Lazarus was buried and told the people to roll away the stone covering the opening. This was not a good idea! Lazarus had been dead four days, and his body would smell! But Jesus knew what He was doing.

So they took away the stone. And Jesus lifted up his eyes and said, "Father, I thank you that you have heard me. I knew that you always hear me, but I said this on account of the people standing around, that they may believe that you sent me." (John 11:41–42)

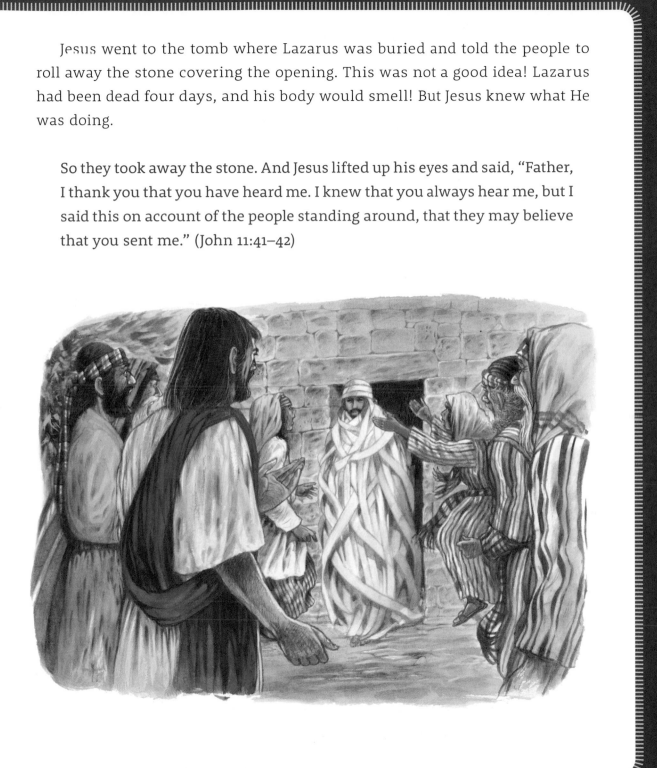

Then Jesus commanded Lazarus to come out of the tomb . . . and Lazarus did! Can you imagine how much joy there was then! There must have been laughing and hugging and . . . there should have been an amazed awe at the power of Jesus.

Jesus could have kept Lazarus from dying. Then Lazarus' sisters and friends would not have suffered so much sadness. He let them suffer because He had something better for them. They needed to believe that Jesus was God's Son. They needed a strong faith in the power, love, and goodness of God.

Suffering teaches us to trust God more. When we suffer, we realize that we need God. We need the strength He promises His children. We need Him to be with us in a scary or hard time, and we need Him to fight for us.

God "does not willingly afflict or grieve the children of men." He does not like to see us suffer. But He will cause suffering when He knows that we need it. Paul, the apostle, understood:

> For we do not want you to be ignorant, brothers, of the affliction we experienced in Asia. For we were so utterly burdened beyond our strength that we despaired of life itself. Indeed, we felt that we had received the sentence of death. But that was to make us rely not on ourselves but on God who raises the dead. (2 Corinthians 1:8–9)

Paul saw God's good purpose in his suffering. Paul needed to learn to depend on God. He knew God would not bring unnecessary suffering into his life. God always has a purpose for our suffering. Will you believe that God's promise is true—not to bring unnecessary suffering into the lives of His children?

We don't always like to do the things that are good for us. You would probably rather play than do your homework, but it is important to learn what you need. It is more fun to stay up at night than to go to bed, but sleep is necessary. Would you rather have things easy and pleasant, or learn the things you must learn? Suffering sometimes is needed to teach us really important lessons. The best thing to learn—to really know—is that Jesus is God's Son, and to have faith in the power, love, and goodness of God.

LEARNING TO TRUST GOD

✢ Read 1 Corinthians 1:8–9 again. Then read 2 Corinthians 1:3–4. How does Paul describe God in 2 Corinthians 1:3? What other purpose for suffering does Paul give? What kind of comfort might God have given Paul when he was suffering?

✢ Read Lamentations 3:31–33. Then read Lamentations 3:22–23. What does this tell you about God and His promises in suffering to His children? Write out Lamentations 3:32–33 on an index card and put it in your "God's Promises" box.

✢ *Activity:* Do you know someone who is suffering? Ask God to show you a way your family can comfort this person. Then bring comfort to that person.

Walking with You in Trials . . . to the Reward

Suppose you lived in a tired, worn-out cabin on the side of a mountain. The door sags and the wind whistles through the cracks. There is a small leak in the roof, and the water in the sink is orange. But the cabin is mostly dry and mostly warm.

One day a letter comes. Your very best friend, who loves you very much, has built you a beautiful mansion on top of another mountain! It is surrounded by a lovely garden next to a dancing stream. Best of all, your friend is living in the mansion, so you can be with him every day.

But there are some valleys to go through, rivers to cross, and even thorn bushes to push through to get to the mansion. And, of course, you must climb the mountain. But you know at the top is the beautiful mansion . . . and your friend.

Life is like this little story. Right now we are in the little cabin of earth. But if you are a Christian, you are walking toward a beautiful home in heaven . . . and Jesus. On the way, there are valleys of disappointments, rivers of sorrow, and mountains of problems. But there are also some wide-open meadows of joy.

God has made a promise for His children to hold on to when they walk through hard times:

> When you pass through the waters, I will be with you;
>   and through the rivers, they shall not overwhelm you;
> when you walk through fire you shall not be burned,
>   and the flame shall not consume you. (Isaiah 43:2)

What does this verse mean by "rivers" and "fire"? They are not real rivers or fire but troubles, sorrows, and hard times. God has not promised that Christians will not have troubles. He has promised to be with us and help us in hard times. And He has promised us a reward at the end:

Blessed is the man who remains steadfast under trial, for when he has stood the test he will receive the crown of life, which God has promised to those who love him. (James 1:12)

What test do you think James is talking about? He is talking about the test of your faith. Will it be strong? Will you keep believing in Jesus and His promises,

even in hard times? Will you keep loving and obeying God until the end of your life? If so, there will be a great reward—life forever in heaven with Jesus, the very best friend of all.

The Bible tells us of Stephen, a man who stayed strong until the end.[1] Stephen was preaching to the Jewish leaders,[2] showing them their sin. This made them very mad! They shouted at him and covered their ears so they could not hear him. Then, do you know what they did in their anger? They dragged Stephen out of the city and threw stones at him.

1. Acts 7:54–60
2. You may need to explain to your child that in the New Testament the Israelites are called the Jews.

And as they were stoning Stephen, he called out, "Lord Jesus, receive my spirit." And falling to his knees he cried out with a loud voice, "Lord, do not hold this sin against them." And when he had said this, he fell asleep.[3] (Acts 7:59–60)

Where was God when all this was happening? He was right there with Stephen. When Stephen passed through the waters and walked through the fire, God was with him. God gave Stephen the courage to preach boldly, the faith to keep believing in Jesus, the grace to forgive the people who killed him, and the sure hope of his reward in heaven. God was faithful to His promise to be with His children in the hard times.

Stephen was steadfast even in the hardest trial, the greatest testing of his faith. "Steadfast" means he was strong—he didn't give up. He kept trusting Jesus.

God made Stephen sure of the end—the reward of life forever in heaven with Jesus. Stephen could stand strong because he knew the promised reward would soon be his.

If you are a Christian, troubles and hard times will come into your life. But God has promised to be with you and to give you life forever in heaven with Jesus if you remain steadfast. Remembering this wonderful promise can help you walk through the waters and finish life well.

Little troubles get us ready for big troubles and make us strong. They teach us to be steadfast. When we have little troubles, we need to remember that God is helping us become strong.

Count it all joy, my brothers, when you meet trials of various kinds, for you know that the testing of your faith produces steadfastness. (James 1:2–3)

3. Your child may need to understand that "fell asleep" means that Stephen died.

LEARNING TO TRUST GOD

✛ Read 2 Corinthians 4:17–18. Look up any words you don't know. Why does Paul call our troubles "light" and "momentary"? What does this verse tell us to do in hard times?

✛ Write out Isaiah 43:2 and James 1:2–3, 12 on an index card and put it in your "God's Promises" box. God gives us little troubles to get us ready for bigger troubles. Thank God for the little troubles that are making you stronger.

✛ *Activity:* The time to get ready for hard times is before they happen. With your family, decide on something you can do to make you strong. Then do it.

Deliverance from Trouble

Have you ever had a broken zipper—one that sort of works? Sometimes it goes part way up before it gets stuck. Sometimes it zips up, but then it won't go down. Sometimes the teeth split so there is a hole. It still works some of the time, buts not the way it should.

That is the way things are in this world. When Adam and Eve disobeyed God in the garden of Eden, sin came into God's perfect world. It wasn't perfect anymore. Things still work . . . but not the way they should, because the world is broken.

In this broken world, where things don't work like they should, there will be problems, troubles, and sorrows. That is what life in a broken world is like. It is like that for everyone . . . even for Christians who love God.

But God has given promises to His children about being in this broken world. Can you think of any of these promises? Maybe you remember about how all things work for good, or that God will be with us when we go through the waters, or some other wonderful promise of God. Here is another one:

> Many are the afflictions of the righteous,
> but the Lord delivers him out of them all. (Psalm 34:19)

To understand this verse, we need to know what the big words mean:

- Afflictions are troubles or problems.
- The righteous are those who trust Jesus to pay for their sins, and live to follow and obey Him.
- Deliver means save or rescue.

Can you say Psalm 34:19 in your own words now?

Christians will have many troubles, but God will rescue them from every one. Can you think of some people God rescued from their troubles? Maybe you thought of Joseph who God saved from the pit and from prison, Daniel who was in the lions' den, or Peter when the angel opened the jail doors. What about Shadrach, Meshach, and Abednego, who would not bow down to the idol? What trouble did they have?

They had a choice. They could bow to the idol or they would be thrown into a fiery furnace. Do you remember what they told the king?

If this be so, our God whom we serve is able to deliver us from the burning fiery furnace, and he will deliver us out of your hand, O king. But if not, be it known to you, O king, that we will not serve your gods or worship the golden image that you have set up. (Daniel 3:17–18)

Shadrach, Meshach, and Abednego would not give up. They were steadfast. They trusted in God and in His promise to deliver them.

This made King Nebuchadnezzar really angry! He ordered the furnace to be made hotter, and hotter, and hotter . . . seven times hotter than it had been. It was so hot that when the soldiers opened the doors to throw Shadrach, Meshach, and Abednego into the furnace, the soldiers were burned to death.

Into this burning fiery furnace went Shadrach, Meshach, and Abednego. But they did not go alone. God was with them.

King Nebuchadnezzar watched to see what would happen. Would their God deliver them, or would Shadrach, Meshach, and Abednego burn in the furnace?

When the righteous cry for help, the Lord hears
    and delivers them out of all their troubles. (Psalm 34:17)

Shadrach, Meshach, and Abednego were delivered from their troubles. They were not burned in the furnace. They didn't even smell like smoke! And the troublesome idol wouldn't be a problem anymore. When King Nebuchadnezzar saw that God rescued Shadrach, Meshach, and Abednego, he made a new law. Anyone who did not show respect to the God of Israel would be punished.

God delivered Shadrach, Meshach, and Abednego from trouble by taking away their problems. But God does not always deliver in the same way. Sometimes He delivers us by giving us the faith and strength to go through hard times. Other times, He delivers His people when they die. Then all their problems are over. Whatever way God rescues His people is the best way for them.

The Lord will rescue me from every evil deed and bring me safely into his heavenly kingdom. To him be the glory forever and ever. Amen. (2 Timothy 4:18)

LEARNING TO TRUST GOD

✦ Read 2 Timothy 4:14–18. What was Paul's trouble? How did God rescue him?

✦ Write out Psalm 23:17, 19 on an index card and put it in your "God's Promises" box. Think of some other people God rescued. How did He deliver them? Thank God for His promise to deliver His people.

✦ *Activity:* God's greatest rescue to man was when He sent His Son to die for our sins. Are you trusting in Jesus alone for your rescue? Read "Ten Essential Truths"[1] again and then explain them to mom or dad.

1. Found in the Appendix.

Joy Comes with the Morning!

What is your favorite circus act? Suppose a circus is coming to town. Most of your friends are going, and everyone is excited! You are excited, too, until you find out that your parents weren't able to get tickets because they were sold out. You are so disappointed. You really wanted to go to the circus, and now you can't.

The day of the big circus comes, and you just wish it were over. All day long, the kids in school are talking about the circus and what acts they are excited about seeing. When you get home, your mom offers you a plate of cookies. Even cookies don't look good to you today. But your mom made them for you, so you take a cookie.

As you pick up the cookie you see . . . a *circus ticket!* Immediately your *sorrow* turns to *joy!* What do you think you would do?

In the Bible, there are many "sorrow turns to joy" times. Can you think of any? Can you imagine the *joy* when the prodigal son returned home? Or when Jacob saw his son, Joseph, again? Or when the lame man at the temple was healed by Peter and John? Or when Peter showed up at the door when the Christians were praying for his release from jail? How about the joy Christians will have when Jesus returns and they meet Him in the sky?

All of these are examples of God keeping His promise:

Weeping may tarry for the night, but joy comes with the morning. (Psalm 30:5)

It is not always night. The night ends, and then day comes. For the Christian, times of sorrow don't last forever . . . and joy comes again. In sad times, remember that the story isn't over yet.

The disciples were sad, because they knew Jesus was going away. Jesus understood their sadness, but He also knew that **"joy comes with the morning"**:

Truly, truly, I say to you, you will weep and lament, but the world will rejoice. You will be sorrowful, but your sorrow will turn into joy . . . . You have sorrow now, but I will see you again, and your hearts will rejoice, and no one will take your joy from you. (John 16:20, 22)

Jesus knew the end of the story. He knew that God turns our sadness into joy.

What if you were there on Good Friday when Jesus was brought to Pilate? How would you feel? What would you think? Would you remember that "joy comes with the morning"? In the midst of the story:

The crowd is yelling, "Crucify Him!" . . . *but the story isn't over yet.*

The soldiers jam a crown of thorns on Jesus' head . . . but the story isn't over yet.

They spit on Jesus and beat him . . . but the story isn't over yet.[1]

God's only Son is nailed to a cross . . . but the story isn't over yet.

The crowd mocked Jesus, "King of the Jews" . . . but the story isn't over yet!

They yelled insults at Him . . . **but the story isn't over yet!**

The soldiers divided up His clothing . . . **but the story isn't over yet!**

"It is finished" . . . His breathing stops . . . **but the story isn't over yet!**

The Savior of the world is laid in a tomb . . . **BUT THE STORY ISN'T OVER YET.**

Mary and the disciples walk away in deep sadness . . . **BUT THE STORY ISN'T OVER YET!**

Weeping may tarry for the night . . . **BUT THE STORY ISN'T OVER YET!**

JOY COMES WITH THE MORNING!

On Sunday, Mary Magdalene stood outside the tomb weeping. She stooped to look inside the tomb. . . . Seeing two angels, she said, "They have taken away my Lord, and I do not know where they have laid him" (John 20:13).

Then she turned around and saw Jesus, but she didn't know it was Jesus . . . until He said her name, "Mary." Jesus was alive! He rose from the dead! Joy flooded over Mary, wave after wave of JOY! "Weeping may tarry for the night, but joy comes with the morning!"

The times of weeping are only for "a night." They will pass here on earth, and some day in heaven they will be no more. We need to remember in the middle of the story that *the story isn't over yet.*

---

1. Encourage your child to repeat *but the story isn't over yet* after each incident.

Is there some sadness in your life or some trouble? If you are a child of God, remember that the story isn't over yet. Remind yourself of God's promise that joy comes with the morning.

> Why are you cast down, O my soul,
>   and why are you in turmoil within me?
> Hope in God; for I shall again praise him,
>   my salvation and my God. (Psalm 42:11)

LEARNING TO TRUST GOD

✤ Read the story of the resurrection in John 20:1–18. Try to imagine the joy the disciples and Mary felt. What might it have looked like?

✤ Write out Psalms 30:5 and 42:11 on an index card and put it in your "God's Promises" box. With your family, make a list of "sorrows turned to joy" in the Bible and in your lives. Thank God for His precious promise to His children.

✤ *Activity:* Do you know someone who is in a time of sadness? How can your family encourage that person? Pray for him, and then do something to encourage him.

Life . . . Forever

What is the difference between a plastic fork and a metal fork? The plastic fork is just *temporary*. It is to be used for just a little while. It doesn't last. After you use it, you often throw it away. But a metal fork is lasting. You can use it always—day after day.

When Jesus came to earth, that was temporary, too. He came just for a little while. His real home was in heaven. Jesus came to die to pay for the sins of those who trust in Him. After He rose from the dead, He would return home to heaven.

The disciples didn't really understand this. They were sad when Jesus told them He was going away.[1] They didn't want Jesus to go away. But Jesus knew that they would only be apart *temporarily*—just for a little while. One day they would be together always—day after day, *forever!*

But the disciples were sad. They only saw the "weeping that tarries for the night." So Jesus told them about the "joy in the morning":

In my Father's house are many rooms. If it were not so, would I have told you that I go to prepare a place for you? And if I go and prepare a place for you, I will come again and will take you to myself, that where I am you may be also. (John 14:2–3)

What wonderful promise was Jesus making in these verses? Jesus would leave, but He was going to make a place for them in heaven where they would be with Him forever! This is Jesus' promise to everyone who is truly trusting in Him.

And this is the promise that he made to us—eternal life. (1 John 2:25)

1. John 13:31–38

Jesus promised the disciples and everyone who is truly trusting in Him eternal life in heaven. Eternal life goes on forever and ever . . . and ever . . . and ever . . . and never stops. In heaven we will always be with Jesus. There will be no sadness, sickness, or pain there. And no "weeping that tarries for the night," because it is always morning:

And the city has no need of sun or moon to shine on it, for the glory of God gives it light, and its lamp is the Lamb. By its light will the nations walk, and the kings of the earth will bring their glory into it, and its gates will never be shut by day—and there will be no night there. (Revelation 21:23–25)

There is always pure joy in heaven! And the greatest joy will be living forever with Jesus.

Do you know anyone who has died as a believer and is now in heaven with Jesus? Can you imagine how very joyful that person must be? Heaven is a truly wonderful place, but not everyone who dies will go to heaven.

A rich young man asked Jesus, "Good Teacher, what must I do to inherit eternal life?" (Luke 18:18). What do you think Jesus told him? Jesus reminded him of the Ten Commandments—"Do not commit adultery, Do not murder, Do not steal, Do not bear false witness, Honor your father and mother" (Luke 18:20).[2] The young man said he had kept all these commandments.

> And Jesus, looking at him, loved him, and said to him, "You lack one thing: go, sell all that you have and give to the poor, and you will have treasure in heaven; and come, follow me." (Mark 10:21)

Jesus was telling the rich young man that he must love God more than anything else. What do you think the young man did? He went away sad, because he was very rich.

The one commandment the rich young man could not keep was the first one— "You shall have no other gods before me" (Exodus 20:3). He loved his money and all that he could buy with it. His money was like a god to him. It was more important than loving God with all his soul, strength, and mind.

Every one of us has the same struggle. Will we love God most of all . . . or will we love other things more? For God's promise of life forever in heaven to be ours, we must trust in Christ and in his words that point out our sin. What do you love most of all? Would you walk away sad like the young man, or would you trust in Jesus and believe His word and receive the greatest treasure of all—living forever in heaven with Jesus?

2. You may need to explain adultery to your child.

Whoever believes in the Son has eternal life; whoever does not obey the Son shall not see life, but the wrath of God remains on him. (John 3:36)

LEARNING TO TRUST GOD

✢ Read the story of the rich young man in Luke 18:18–30. It is easy to say that we would not be like the rich young man, but is that really true? It is very easy for our hearts to love other things more than loving God. What things do you love? Pray that God would be most important in your heart.

✢ Write out John 14:2–3 on an index card and put it in your "God's Promises" box. What do you think it will be like in heaven with Jesus? Thank God for His promise of eternal life.

✢ *Activity:* We all struggle with loving this world, so it is a good practice to keep other things from being too important to us. What is one thing your family could sacrifice for someone else? What is hard about giving this thing up? What does it show you about your heart? With your family, take a step of sacrificial love toward someone else.

God Is Not Slow in Keeping His Promises

When you see your wrapped Christmas presents, is it hard to wait to open them? Why? Waiting is not easy because our hearts are often very impatient. We want to see what is in the presents *now!* But we need to wait because there is a right time to open the gifts.

God's promises are like this. They are gifts from God, and there is a right time for each of them. Sometimes God keeps a promise right away, but other promises are like waiting for our Christmas presents—it seems to take a long time before those promises are kept. But all of God's promises are for sure.

Can you think of any times in the Bible when a person had to wait a long time for God's promise to come about? Abraham waited a long time for baby Isaac. David waited 20 years before he was crowned king of Israel. And Israel waited hundreds of years for the Savior to come. But God kept all of those promises, at just the right time.

Sometimes it seems to us like it is taking God too long to keep His promises, but the Bible says:

> The Lord is not slow to fulfill his promise as some count slowness, but is patient toward you, not wishing that any should perish, but that all should reach repentance. (2 Peter 3:9)

Just as the Jews once waited for Jesus to come, so we are waiting for Jesus to return. We wonder why Jesus hasn't come back yet to bring His people to heaven with Him. But this verse says that God is not slow. He has a reason for waiting. God is patient with man and is giving those who don't love Him time to turn away from sin and turn to Him.

Whenever God waits to keep a promise, He has a good reason for waiting. Maybe you wanted a two-wheeled bike when you were little. But your parents gave you a tricycle first. You had to wait to get the bigger bike. They didn't make you wait because they were slow but because you weren't ready for the big bike. You had to learn some other things first. God knows even better than our parents what we need and when we need it.

Faith is believing God's Word even when God takes a long time to act. It is trusting that God will do what He says He will do, and that it will be the right time when He does it.

God made a promise to Rebekah when she was waiting for Jacob and Esau to be born:

And the Lord said to her, "Two nations are in your womb, and two peoples from within you shall be divided; the one shall be stronger than the other, the older shall serve the younger." (Genesis 25:23)

Esau was a few minutes older than Jacob. So Isaac, like all fathers in Israel, would pass on his blessing to the oldest son. But God's promise was for Jacob and his family. Rebekah had a hard time waiting for God to keep

His promise. Instead of trusting God, Rebekah told Jacob to trick his father and steal Esau's blessing. Jacob listened to the bad advice of his mother and did not wait for God to work for him.

Rebekah and Jacob were impatient. They did not trust that God is not slow in keeping His promises, but keeps them at just the right time.

Simeon was an old man, but the Holy Spirit had shown Simeon that he would not die before he saw the Savior. So Simeon waited, trusting God's promise to send a Savior, and trusting that He would see the Savior. When Mary and Joseph brought baby Jesus to the temple, Simeon knew God had kept His promise:

> Lord, now you are letting your servant depart in peace,
>   according to your word;
> for my eyes have seen your salvation. (Luke 2:29–30)

Simeon's waiting was over. God had kept His promise to send Jesus. God's plans are always good and right. And His timing is always perfect.

Do you believe that God is always right? We can wait either trusting God to keep His promise at just the right time, or we can be impatient and sin like Rebekah and Jacob. Waiting is easier if you remember that God is always good and always right.

> I wait for the LORD, my soul waits,
>   and in his word I hope. (Psalm 130:5)

✢ Read Psalm 130:5 again. What does waiting for the Lord look like? What does it mean to hope in God's Word? What would it have looked like for Rebekah to hope in God's Word?

✢ Write out 2 Peter 3:9 on an index card and put it in your "God's Promises" box. How is God patient with you? Thank God for His patience and for His perfect timing.

✢ *Activity:* Ask mom or dad to tell you about a time when they had to wait for God's timing. How can they now see that God's timing was perfect? Make Jell-O®[1] and divide it into two containers. Eat some of the first before it is set; wait for the second until the right time. Why is patience so important?

1. Or you could make Popsicles® or anything else that has to set for a while.

Look Up, Not Down

If you were taking a dog for a walk, would you just put the dog on a leash and then ignore it? What would you do?

You would watch the dog. If it gets too close to the street, you would lead the dog away. If the leash gets tangled in the dog's legs, you would untangle it. You pay attention to what is happening with the dog.

God does the same thing with His promises. He pays attention to them. God told the prophet Jeremiah:

I am watching over my word to perform it. (Jeremiah 1:12)

When God makes a promise, He makes sure that the promise comes true.

Do you remember the promise that God made to Abraham? God said He would make Abraham's family into a great nation. That promise was for Abraham's son Isaac, Isaac's son Jacob, and Jacob's sons. Jacob had 12 sons, but he loved Joseph more the rest and gave him a beautiful coat.

God gave Joseph a promise in a dream. His promise was that Joseph would rule over his brothers. Joseph's brothers did not like Joseph or that he was given a special coat. And they especially did not like that Joseph thought he would rule over them.

Do you remember what Joseph's brothers did to him? They wanted to kill him, but instead they threw him into a pit—a deep, dark hole. When some travelers came by on the way to Egypt, Joseph's brothers sold Joseph to them as a slave.

Now Joseph was far away in Egypt . . . and he was a slave in the house of a man named Potipher. What about God's promise? Did God forget His promise? Joseph was not becoming a great nation, and he was not ruling over anything.

Joseph had a choice. He could look down at himself and complain, saying, "Poor me. This isn't fair! God has forgotten about me." Or he could look up to God and ask with wonder, "What are you up to, God? What great plan do you have, and what part do I have in it?" Joseph chose to trust God, and God blessed him as a slave by giving him important responsibilities.

Then Potipher's wife wanted Joseph to do something wrong, but Joseph wouldn't do it. So she got angry and lied about Joseph. This time Joseph wasn't thrown into a pit . . . he was thrown in jail! What about God's promise? Did God forget His promise?

Once again, Joseph had a choice. He could look down at himself and at his situation and complain. Or he could look up to God and trust that God had a good plan. Do you know what Joseph chose?

Joseph chose to trust God, and God blessed him in prison, too. Soon he was put in charge of many things in the prison. After some time, a servant of the king of Egypt was thrown in prison. Joseph helped the servant to understand a dream. He told the servant that the dream meant the servant would get out of prison and serve the king (Pharaoh) again. Then Joseph asked the servant to tell Pharaoh about him.

Joseph waited two more years in prison . . . but God is not slow in keeping His promises. He knew that Joseph had things to learn in prison—how to be in charge of things and how to be a better man. Again, Joseph could look down and complain, "Why do I have to be here so long? God has forgotten His promise." Or he could look up to God with trust and say, "God, you have a good plan. You know what you are doing. You always keep your promise. You are watching over your Word to make it true."

Do you know what happened next? Pharaoh had a special dream from God, but no one knew what it meant. Pharaoh was upset that no one could help him understand his dream. Then God made Pharaoh's servant remember about Joseph.

When Joseph was brought to the king, God helped him to know what Pharaoh's dream meant. Pharaoh was so grateful that he gave Joseph a very important job. Pharaoh put Joseph in charge of the whole land of Egypt!

This was God's perfect plan, because soon there was no food in the land where Joseph's family lived. But God had put Joseph in just the right place at just the right time to help his family to get food. God was watching over His promise to make from Abraham a great nation, and He was taking care of Jacob's family so they had food to eat. God had a good plan, and God made sure that every part of it happened.

God has a good plan for all His children. If you are a Christian, God has a good plan for your life. He is making sure His plan works well. So when something happens that you don't like, you can know that it is part of God's good plan. You can either look down at your situation and complain about what is happening to you, or you can look up to God who always keeps His promises, always watches over what He has promised, and always makes sure that His plans always work right. Will you look down or up?

As I have planned,
    so shall it be,
and as I have purposed,
    so shall it stand. (Isaiah 14:24)

LEARNING TO TRUST GOD

✢ Read Genesis 45:4–11 and Genesis 50:15–21. What does this tell you about trusting God?

✢ Write out Jeremiah 1:12 on an index card and put it in your "God's Promises" box. Thank God that He can be trusted to keep His promises.

✢ *Activity:* Pick a night to go outside and look at the stars with your family. Can you count them? Remind yourself of God's promise to give Abraham a bigger family than he could ever count. Remember that just as God kept His promise to Abraham, so He keeps His promises to all His children. That's why we should look up, not down.

Standing on God's Promises

Have you ever been on a tire swing? Was it fun? Suppose there was a tire swing that swung out over a big lake, and two boys took a ride on it. One boy was scared . . . to . . . death. All he could see was all that water. He wondered how deep it was, and whether the rope knot would hold. He couldn't wait to get off the swing.

The other boy saw three stocky men test the tree limb. He saw them tie three knots in the rope. Then all three of them jerked on the rope and tested the knot with the full weight of their three bodies. When the boy got on the swing he looked at the big lake, but he remembered the limb and the knot. The limb was strong. The knot was sure. The boy had so much fun on the tire swing, taking turn after turn.

Why did the boys have different experiences? Both rode on the same tire swing. It had not changed. The difference was what they put their minds on and the trust each boy had in the swing.

The Bible tells us a story about 10 men who were like the boy who was scared and two men who had complete trust and confidence. Do you know who they were?

God had promised Israel a good land "flowing with milk and honey" (Exodus 3:8; Leviticus 20:24). This meant it was rich, full of grass for their animals, good land for farming, and plenty of everything they needed. But first the Israelites had to fight and defeat the people living there.

So Moses sent 12 spies to check out the land and the people. The spies came back with their report, and the land was exactly as God had promised:

And they told him, "We came to the land to which you sent us. It flows with milk and honey, and this is its fruit. However, the people who dwell in the land are strong, and the cities are fortified and very large. And besides, we saw the descendants of Anak there." (Numbers 13:27–28)

All the men saw the same land, but not all of them trusted God's promise. Not all of them saw the greatness and faithfulness of God. So they had two different ideas about the same thing:

But Caleb quieted the people before Moses and said, "Let us go up at once and occupy it, for we are well able to overcome it." Then the men who had gone up with him said, "We are not able to go up against the people, for they are stronger than we are." (Numbers 13:30–31)

Most of the spies saw only how big the people were. Only Joshua and Caleb believed that God always keeps His promises and would give them the land if they obeyed Him.[1] They knew God is stronger than the people of the land. Joshua and Caleb knew what David would later write about in the Psalms:

1. Numbers 14:7–9

This God—his way is perfect;

   the word of the LORD proves true;

   he is a shield for all those who take refuge in him. (Psalm 18:30)

What do you think the people of Israel believed? The Bible says that they "raised a loud cry, and the people wept that night" (Numbers 14:1). They did not trust God or His promise. They wanted to return to Egypt where they had been slaves. They were sure they would be killed or taken captive if they tried to fight for the land.

But Joshua and Caleb stood strong, believing in God and His promise. They refused to believe the lie that God does not keep His promises. They had strong trust in His power and faithfulness. They were like the boy who thought about the strength of the knot and the tree limb and was not afraid of falling into the lake.

Because the people of Israel did not trust in God or His promise, they lost the chance to live in the good land God had promised them. The consequence for not trusting God was that the Israelites had to wander in the wilderness for 40 years—until every one of them except Joshua and Caleb died.

You have read about the wonderful promises of God in this book. They are presents from God to His children. We do not deserve them, but God gives them because He is good. God keeps every one of His promises because He is all-powerful, all-knowing, all-loving, and unselfish. He does not lie, and He never forgets anything.

God's promises have not changed. Just like the rope swing, they have been tested and found to be sure and strong. Not one of them has ever been broken.

If you are a child of God through adoption by faith in Jesus, these good promises are yours. When hard times come, all of God's promises will be a strong, sure rope for you. Will you trust God and believe His promises like Joshua and Caleb? Or will you be like the other 10 spies? Will you *stand* on the promises of God—not budging, but holding firmly to the sure promises of God? Will you say with confidence:

I believe that I shall look upon the goodness of the Lord
in the land of the living!
Wait for the Lord;
be strong, and let your heart take courage;
wait for the Lord! (Psalm 27:13–14)

LEARNING TO TRUST GOD

✛ Read Numbers 14:1–35. Why didn't the people believe God's promise? What was the consequence to them?

✛ Read Psalm 27. What was David waiting for? How do verses 13 and 14 show that David was trusting God? Write out Psalm 18:30 and Psalm 27:13–14 on an index card and put it in your "God's Promises" box. Thank God that His Word is always true, and that He promises good to His people.

✛ *Activity:* Read all the promise cards in your box. Talk about what it looks like in your life to trust in these promises. Sing the hymn "Standing on the Promises of God" with your family. Keep your "God's Promises" box and read the promises often. When you are scared, sad, or having a hard time, remind yourself of these wonderful promises.

Appendix
Ten Essential Truths[1]

Truth One
God is the sovereign Creator of all things.

Scripture

Psalm 19:1; Psalm 22:28; Psalm 24:1; Isaiah 44:24

Implication

God made you. You belong to God. God is your Ruler.

Truth Two
God created people for His glory.

Scripture

Psalm 29:1–2; Isaiah 43:6–7; 1 Corinthians 10:31

Implication

God created you to know, trust, and love Him most of all.

Truth Three
God is holy and righteous.

Scripture

Leviticus 19:2, 37; Deuteronomy 32:4; Romans 7:12

Implication

God is holy and righteous. God's commands are holy and righteous. You must obey God's commands all the time.

---

1. Truths excerpted from: Sally Michael, Jill Nelson, and Bud Burk, *Helping Children to Understand the Gospel* (Minneapolis: Children Desiring God and Bethlehem Baptist Church, 2009), 37–85. Used by permission. For a more detailed explanation of these essential truths and child-appropriate teaching of them, see the *Helping Children to Understand the Gospel* booklet, available at www.childrendesiringGOD.org.

Truth Four
Man is sinful.

Scripture
Romans 3:10–18, 20, 23

Implication
You have disobeyed God's commands. You are a sinner.

Truth Five
God is just, and is right to punish sin.

Scripture
Isaiah 59:2; Romans 1:18; Romans 6:23 (Note: read only the first part of Romans 6:23 at this time: "The wages of sin is death.")

Implication
You deserve God's punishment of death and hell. You are helpless to save yourself.

Truth Six
God is merciful. He is kind to undeserving sinners.

Scripture
Psalm 145:8; Ephesians 2:8–9

Implication
You must depend on God's mercy in order to be saved.

Truth Seven
Jesus is God's holy and righteous Son.

Scripture
John 1:1, 14; I Timothy 1:15

Implication
Jesus came into the world to save you.

Truth Eight
God put the punishment of sinners on Jesus, so that His righteousness might be put on them.

Scripture

Isaiah 53:5; Romans 5:8; 2 Corinthians 5:21; 1 Peter 2:24

Implication

Jesus died on the cross to be punished in your place.

Truth Nine
God offers the free gift of salvation to those who repent and believe in Jesus.

Scripture

Mark 1:15; John 3:16–17; Acts 4:12; Ephesians 2:8–9

Implication

God tells you to believe in Jesus and repent of your sins, and you will be saved.

Truth Ten
Those who trust in Jesus will live to please Him and will receive the promise of eternal life—enjoying God forever in heaven.

Scripture

Luke 9:23; John 11:25; 1 John 2:15; Psalm 16:11

Implication

If you are trusting in Jesus for your salvation, you must follow Him. Jesus has promised that when you die He will bring you to heaven to live with God and enjoy Him forever.

Praise for *God's Promises*

This book is a powerful expression of biblical truth for children. Our church has used the Sunday school curriculum based on the same material. Without fail, it has deepened the faith of teacher and child. Now in book format, these powerful concepts can easily be used in a home setting. Children deserve this kind of foundation upon which to build their faith.

>   —TONY KUMMER, children's pastor; founder of Ministry-To-Children.com

Sally Michael paints a clear and wondrous picture of God's promises. It thrilled my soul as I read it, and I can't wait to teach it to my grandchildren! She does not sugarcoat any of the more difficult promises, but explains them in a way that shows a high view of God and gives people, even little people, great confidence and hope in what God is doing. *God's Promises* is an amazing teaching tool for parents and those teaching children in church settings. I highly recommend it.

>   —MARTHA PEACE, biblical counselor; author of *The Excellent Wife*; coauthor of *The Faithful Parent*

What a blessing for kids to grow up understanding God's varied promises—conditional or unconditional, given to one individual, to God's people, or to all humanity. This book is clear, profound, helpful, and at every point grounded with faith and confidence in *who God is*. A tremendous resource!

>   —ELIZABETH GROVES, Lecturer in Old Testament, Westminster Seminary

The family is the place for dazzling kids with the glories of God. *God's Promises* is a great tool for doing just that. This engaging, attractively illustrated book teaches not only the promises of the Bible, but also the character of the God who makes and keeps his promises. Avoiding theological triteness, Sally Michael distinguishes between conditional and unconditional promises, broadly focused and more pointedly intended promises. Along the way are thoughtful questions and meaningful activities for kids. If you want to bring the delights of God to your children, get this book.

>   —TEDD TRIPP, President, Shepherding the Heart Ministries

children desiring God

This storybook was adapted from *Faithful to All His Promises*, an upper-elementary Sunday school curriculum published by Children Desiring God. If you would like to further explore the promises of God or other aspects of His counsel with your student, resources are available from Children Desiring God.

Children Desiring God is a nonprofit ministry that Sally Michael and her husband David Michael helped to establish in the late 1990s. CDG publishes God-centered, Bible-saturated, Christ-exalting resources to help parents and churches spiritually train their children in the hope that the next generation will see and embrace Jesus Christ as the One who saves and satisfies the soul. Resources include nursery through youth curriculum (see sequence chart on following page), parenting booklets, and Bible memory resources. Free parenting and Christian education training audio lectures are also available online.

Please contact us if we can partner with you for the joy of the next generation.

childrendesiringGOD.org
cdg@desiringGOD.org

SUNDAY SCHOOL	
Nursery	**A Sure Foundation** A Philosophy and Curriculum for Ministry to Infants and Toddlers
Preschool	**He Established a Testimony** Old Testament Stories for Young Children
Preschool	**He Has Spoken By His Son** New Testament Stories for Young Children

	SUNDAY SCHOOL	MIDWEEK
K	**Jesus, What a Savior!** A Study for Children on Redemption	**He Has Been Clearly Seen** A Study for Children on Seeing and Delighting in God's Glory
1	**The ABCs of God** A Study for Children on the Greatness and Worth of God	**I Stand in Awe** A Study for Children on the Bible
2	**Faithful to All His Promises** A Study for Children on the Promises of God	(Children Desiring God will announce plans for this title in the future.)
3	**In the Beginning . . . Jesus** A Chronological Study for Children on Redemptive History	**The Way of the Wise** A Study for Children on Wisdom and Foolishness
4	**To Be Like Jesus** A Study for Children on Following Jesus	**I Will Build My Church** A Study for Children on the Church (future release)
5	**How Majestic Is Your Name** A Study for Children on the Names and Character of God	**Pour Out Your Heart before Him** A Study for Children on Prayer and Praise in the Psalms (future release)
6	**My Purpose Will Stand** A Study for Children on the Providence of God	**Fight the Good Fight** A Study for Children on Persevering in Faith
7	**Your Word Is Truth** A Study for Youth on Seeing All of Life through the Truth of Scripture	**Abiding in Jesus** A Study for Youth on Trusting Jesus and Encouraging Others
8	**Teach Me Your Way** A Study for Youth on Surrender to Jesus and Submission to His Way	**Rejoicing in God's Good Design** A Study for Youth on Biblical Manhood and Womanhood (future release)

Also by Sally Michael

God's Names

SALLY MICHAEL

"The God she sees, savors, and sets forth here is unabashedly big." —John Piper

When you want to get to know someone, where do you start? How do you introduce yourself?

Usually you start with someone's name.

God knows this—and he doesn't have just one name to share with us, either! The Bible gives us many names for God and tells us what they all mean. And when we learn a new name for God, we learn something new about him, too!

This book is for you and your children to read together. Every chapter teaches something new and helps put you—and your children—on the right track in your relationship with God.

God has left his names with his people so they can know him . . . and through these pages your children can know him too.

"The God Sally sees, savors, and sets forth here is unabashedly big. Not distant and uncaring. But great enough to make his caring count."
—JOHN PIPER, Author; Pastor for Preaching and Vision, Bethlehem Baptist Church, Minneapolis, Minnesota

"Sally Michael creatively helps parents to lead their children through a fun and fascinating exploration of the various ways God's names reveal the beauty and power of his character and actions."
—JUSTIN TAYLOR, Managing Editor, *ESV Study Bible*

"Grandparents and parents and all the extended family, as well as those who make up the church of the living God, all have a divine unction to pass along God's truth to the hearts of our children! Sally Michael has given us an excellent tool in *God's Names* to do just that!"
—DOROTHY PATTERSON, General Editor, *The Woman's Study Bible*; Professor of Theology in Women's Studies, Southwestern Baptist Theological Seminary

Youth Fiction from P&R

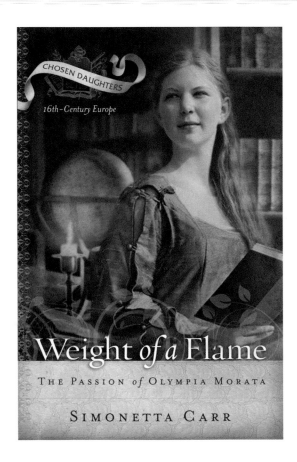

The Chosen Daughters series highlights the lives of ordinary women who by God's grace accomplish extraordinary things.

"With the precision of a scholar and the heart of a storyteller, Simonetta Carr brings to life the story of Olympia Morata, a daughter of the Italian Reformation."

—ERIC LANDRY, Executive Director of White Horse, Inc., home of *Modern Reformation* and the *White Horse Inn* radio program

Also in the Chosen Daughters series:

Against the Tide: The Valor of Margaret Wilson, by Hope Irvin Marston

A Cup of Cold Water: The Compassion of Nurse Edith Cavell, by Christine Farenhorst

Dr. Oma: The Healing Wisdom of Countess Juliana von Stolberg, by Ethel Herr

Wings like a Dove: The Courage of Queen Jeanne D'Albret, by Christine Farenhorst

Olympia Morata (1526–1555) is her father's finest student and a girl far ahead of her time. A quick tongue and a ready pen are her mind's tools to record her vivid thoughts, poetry, songs, and opinions. Appointed tutor to Duchess Renée's children, Olympia looks forward to a bright future—when suddenly, evil rumors threaten to turn her world upside down. In the midst of it all, a young doctor comes courting. Will their love survive the danger waiting on the other side of the Alps?

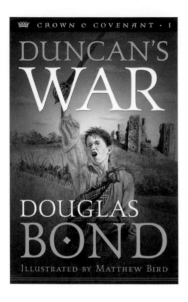 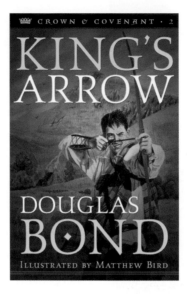 

Young Duncan M'Kethe finds himself caught in the web of Sir James Turner, the former Covenanter turned military leader of the persecutors. Duncan is torn by his hatred of his enemies and his father's instructions to love them. He must be true to King Jesus while attempting to rescue his father.

The Crown & Covenant series follows the lives of the M'Kethe family as they endure persecution in 17th–century Scotland and later flee to colonial America. Douglas Bond weaves together fictional characters and historical figures from Scottish Covenanting history.

"Intrigue. Suspense. High-stakes drama. *Duncan's War* educates and inspires us to look back at heroes of the faith in awe and forward to the return of the King in joy."
   —R. C. SPROUL JR., Director, Highlands Study Center

"Unleashes the reader's imagination—a rip-roaring good yarn."
   —GEORGE GRANT, Director, King's Meadow Study Center

Youth Resources from P&R

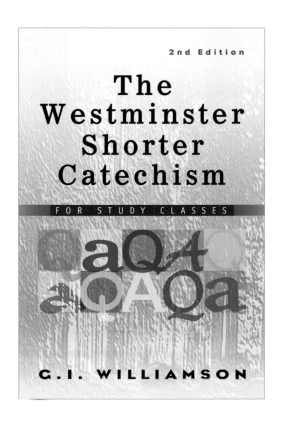

The Westminster Shorter Catechism is unrivaled as a concise and faithful summary of the central teachings of Scripture. For decades G. I. Williamson's study manuals on the Shorter Catechism have served as invaluable tools for instructing young and old in the Reformed system of doctrine.

Now newly typeset in one volume, this illustrated manual offers clear exposition of each of the 107 questions in the Shorter Catechism. Each lesson includes Scripture proofs as well as questions for review or discussion. A valuable aid for group instruction or private study, this volume has been used successfully by homeschoolers, pastors, Sunday school teachers, and parents.

Instructional Children's Fiction from P&R

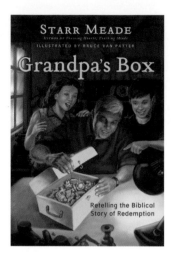

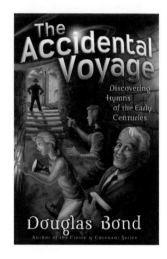

"It was a wooden box, simply made. 'I guess you could call it my war chest,' Grandpa said. As the children peered into the box, they saw many small figures—animals, people, and objects of all kinds. A number of them were carved from wood."

Learn along with Marc and Amy as Grandpa shares his stories of the great war we are all fighting. See how his special box of wooden carvings illustrates the wonderful stories of the Bible.

STARR MEADE, author of the popular *Training Hearts, Teaching Minds*, takes children to a deeper understanding of God's plan of redemption told throughout all of Scripture. Each chapter emphasizes what we learn about God, not just what we learn about individual characters in the Bible.

Follow Mr. Pipes, Annie, and Drew on another exciting adventure through mysterious lands and seas! Ride a moped with Drew through the streets of Rome, explore dark catacombs with Annie, and listen as Mr. Pipes celebrates the hymns of the early centuries. Sail with them all on a schooner bound for . . .

"Just what kind of books are the Mr. Pipes stories? Are they lessons in church history? Guides to family devotions? Unit studies on hymnody and classic ecclesiastical music? Basic theological primers? They are all these. But what is more, they are also delightful tales with memorable characters and intriguing plot twists. These are the kind of books every family is going to want to have and read—and reread."

—GEORGE GRANT, author of *Going Somewhere* and *The Christian Almanac*